ADVANC

"An outstanding book unlike any other, packed with clear and compelling advice and examples that get straight to the point, are easy to apply, and delivered in a personable and digestible way."

KATHY KRENGER

Award-winning international
Chief Communications Officer and Brand Builder

"Addressing the right audience with the right message, at the right time, is critical for any business leader, and more important than ever. This book reinforces that with great examples and validates the importance of enabling a great communications team."

R. MICHAEL MOHAN

Board Chair and former President and COO of Best Buy

"Smart, snappy, insightful, informed by a wealth of personal experience (triumphs and disasters), unflinchingly honest, wise, practical – a superb guide to communicating with a wide range of audiences, from colleagues to the media to the general public. Indispensable both for those facing the cameras and for those preparing them."

BARNEY THOMPSON

Editor and writer at the United Nations,
former journalist and editor at *The Financial Times*

Published by
LID Publishing
An imprint of LID Business Media Ltd.
LABS House, 15-19 Bloomsbury Way,
London, WC1A 2TH, UK

info@lidpublishing.com
www.lidpublishing.com

A member of:

businesspublishersroundtable.com

© Benjamin Thiele-Long, 2025
© LID Business Media Limited, 2025

Printed and bound in Great Britain by Halstan Ltd
ISBN: 978-1-917391-56-6
ISBN: 978-1-917391-57-3 [ebook]

Cover and Page design: Caroline Li

HOW TO BE UTTERLY BRILLIANT

AT PUBLIC SPEAKING, PRESENTING AND TALKING TO THE MEDIA

BENJAMIN THIELE-LONG

MADRID | MEXICO CITY | LONDON
BUENOS AIRES | BOGOTA | SHANGHAI

For Ian

Without whom nothing in the world
would be worth listening to

CONTENTS

PANELS AND PITCHES 146

MEDIA INTERVIEWS 194

It matters not how strait the gate,
How charged with punishments the scroll,
I am the master of my fate,
I am the captain of my soul.

WILLIAM ERNEST HENLEY

INTRODUCTION

I am not perfect at presenting. No one is.

So, what is this book for?

Any public figure you see speaking to the media, presenting to a group or talking at a company town hall would probably change something about their speeches or presentations if they watched them back again.

No matter how experienced they are.

Truly great orators, of any kind, are like stage actors.

Because every rehearsal and every performance is an opportunity to improve and perfect. And then the next play comes along, and they adjust different things.

That is their craft. And that process is what makes them good at what they do.

But unlike trained actors, very few of us are ever really taught how to be a good public speaker or presenter or even how to articulate our ideas in the best, most persuasive way possible.

This book is my way of doing that.

It's a compilation of everything I've learned through my years as both a barrister and a communications consultant, but most importantly a trusted advisor; watching, rehearsing, writing for, cringing at, but most importantly championing the public speakers I've worked with.

I hope this book becomes your trusted guide, always within reaching distance of your desk.

A faithful companion when you don't have tenured speech writers and media consultants, or teams of producers and directors to prepare everything for you. And even if you do, you will *still* learn something from this book.

And I really don't mind if you read the whole book or just one page.

If you take just one thing away, and make one improvement to your public speaking, then this book has been a success.

Above all, it's designed to be a confidence builder.

Because if there is one thing I believe more than anything else, it's this:

> **Everyone can be utterly brilliant at public speaking and presenting.**

The hardest part is structuring what to say and how to say it; that is what this book does.

Part advisor, part champion, I'm here to unlock your potential, show you the way and support everyone who reads and applies what they can, when they can.

So, whether you want to build your confidence at leading a team meeting, or you're preparing for an international broadcast to the UN, this book is my way of both *telling* you that "*you got this*" and *showing* you how to be utterly brilliant at it.

HOW TO USE THIS BOOK

This book is designed as a clear and simple guide, with pithy and practical tools and exercises that will improve and perfect your public speaking skills instantly.

No theoretical exposition. No waffle. No fuss.

Up front are the Golden Rules: three foundational principles I have learned through decades of experience that apply to *every* public speaking event, presentation, pitch, media engagement, you name it.

The rules focus on audience, persuasion and narrative.

They are the foundation needed to frame your approach every time you speak. Even if you don't have long to prepare.

Keep coming back to them. Please.

As composer John Powell said:

> *"Communication works for those who work at it."*

The guide is then divided into aspects of public speaking and presenting, each beginning with three key principles that are meant as an *aide-mémoire* to look at EVERY time you get ready for an event. Each chapter then explores those concepts in more detail, but the principles give you the quick refresher.

The book is also designed deliberately with plenty of space; write notes, jot down your own prompts and include your own examples or shorthand. This should be a living, breathing tool.

And for the PR and communications leaders reading this, keep coming back to it also.

I can guarantee you, from experience, no matter how well prepared you are to advise your spokesperson, you'll forget something.

Use it when preparing materials and use it when you are coaching your spokespeople so both you – and they – have a common language you're both working with.

It will make you a MUCH better advisor to senior leaders.
That is a promise.

Above all, I hope this book becomes your secret weapon, however you use it, such that no speaker takes the mic without having referred back to it *at least* once beforehand.

THE
GOLDEN
RULES

Over the next few pages, I set out the three Golden Rules that underpin every good speech, presentation, pitch or interview.

But far from theoretical exposition, the Golden Rules are the practical foundation you should go to *every* time you have to speak.

Taking the time to apply them is vital, no matter how experienced you are.

Why?

Because every speaking scenario is different and requires a tailored approach.

Every. Single. Scenario.

That's why the Golden Rules are what they are.

They set the direction for what you're going to say and how you're going to say it every time.

Guaranteed.

GOLDEN RULE 1:
COMMUNICATION IS AN AUDIENCE-DEFINED ACTION

The greatest unlock for effective public speaking – or any communication for that matter – is establishing that it is never a one-way process.

This is the core difference between transmitting and communicating.

Motivational speaker Jim Rohn said it best:

> *"The goal of effective communication should be for listeners to say, 'me, too!' versus 'so what?'"*

The vast majority of poor or ineffective public speaking comes from a fundamental failure of understanding the audience and tailoring the content to them.

A few years ago, I attended a two-day conference on business leadership, which had ten guest speakers. They were all doctors or professors of their subject, all of them were professional speakers, and all of them had published a book on their area of expertise.

All things being equal, therefore, you'd expect ten presentations of matching quality and impact.

But to this day I can recall the speakers that delivered an exceptional presentation, with advice and concepts I still retain, and those that did not.

The reason for the delta was stark and simple.

The speakers who excelled were those who had first considered the nature and reason for the audience being there in the first place and then tailored both their content and delivery specifically to the audience's level of expertise and expectations.

Defining your audience:
- If it's a work presentation:
  What's everyone's level of knowledge, and who's making decisions?

- If it's a conference:
  What's the topic of the whole event, and why have people paid to come?

- If it's to a journalist:
  What's the news outlet, who reads it and when is it being published?

Missing this fundamental step is like leaving a magnet by a compass; you'll go off course very quickly.

So, the first question you should always ask yourself is:
"Who exactly am I speaking to?"

Now you need to define *why* you're speaking to them.

GOLDEN RULE 2:
PERSUASION ACHIEVES IRRESISTIBLE OUTCOMES

The second trait every good speaker has in common is that everything they present is done in service of achieving a clear and specific outcome. <u>They are never speaking just for the sake of it.</u>

That means *every* type of presentation needs to be an act of persuasion for it to be effective.

Importantly, being persuasive starts with being crystal clear in your own mind about what outcome you're trying to achieve; usually to influence a belief or a behaviour.

Defining your outcome:
- Your team meeting is not to talk about updates to staffing changes.
  It's to establish team cohesion and adoption of new and improved ways of working.

- Your podcast appearance is not to talk about AI trends.
  It's about demonstrating what AI tech should be applying to their business to remain competitive.

- Your Bloomberg interview is not to share your company performance.
  It's to get people to invest, buy from, or do business with your company.

This is something you *have* to be crystal clear about before you put pen to paper and prepare any talking points, slides or visual elements.

Because once you've established the outcome you want to achieve, you can then ask yourself:

> *"What are the most persuasive ideas, concepts or proof points that will drive the desired outcome I'm seeking?"*

This is what's needed to put together a set of talking points and materials that are going to be deliberate, cohesive and *all* in service of a clearly defined outcome. Without it, you'll just have a collection of ideas and statements which might be interesting, but not necessarily persuasive.

It's a process that *must* be done backwards and intentionally by you so it can be done forwards and easily by your audience.

Persuasion is NEVER about forcing a decision on someone. Persuasion is always about setting the path that leads your audience naturally, effortlessly and willingly to your desired outcome.

And if you do it right, you'll make your desired outcome *irresistible* with everything you say.

Because the most persuasive path to an irresistible outcome is always the one that is *easiest to follow*, and the one that simply makes good sense precisely because you've made it so.

GOLDEN RULE 3:
SET THE PATH WITH A COMPELLING NARRATIVE

Now that you have a clear understanding of your audience and the outcome you're trying to achieve, you need to bind it all together cohesively and clearly.

A list of statements or facts, no matter how valid, is unlikely to persuade or inspire anyone.

Why not?

Because humans are storytellers. The first languages and communities were developed through storytelling. There is something in our DNA that wires us to take interest and proactively engage both emotionally and mentally in a good story.

Just think of your favourite film or book that you've probably watched or read multiple times – you know what's going to happen, but the journey is what compels you.

Think about the journey you want to take this specific audience on and how to connect all the parts of what you need to say; that will give you the framework for the most compelling and irresistible version of what you have to say.

It's your first *Financial Times* interview on company performance as CEO to bolster investment at a time of growth.

Defining your narrative:

- *What makes the company's growth story to date compelling, where is it going, why is this a moment of significant change, and what does that direction promise?*

- It's a presentation about a new project you want the team to support or fund: *What is the competitive landscape in this space, where is the opportunity, why is the progress to date significant, and what makes the end point critical?*

- It's a TED Talk about how you created your nonprofit business and raised awareness of a specific issue: *What were you doing first, what experience did you have, how did it change your mindset, what were the trials in the process, what was the success you achieved and why?*

A narrative can be simple or complex, but it underpins how everything fits together in a way that relates to this specific audience.

Putting what you say into a narrative of some kind informs how you'll bring all your points into a cohesive set of ideas. This gives your audience a way to follow you easily and draw them to your irresistible outcome naturally and effortlessly.

Framing everything in a clear and compelling narrative is the most foundational Golden Rule.

Without a narrative, your words are just a set of statements. With a narrative, your words become something people *have* to listen to.

THE GOLDEN POSITIONING SYSTEM

What makes these the Golden Rules?

Because it's the combination of these three things together that will shape what you are going to say and how you're going to say it, regardless of the format.

Just like the GPS technology in a car that sets your direction by the triangulation of three points.

These rules now form your *Golden Positioning System* when it comes to presenting and public speaking.

Every time.

I dare say that having read it out loud, it all seems obvious. But to paraphrase Sherlock Holmes:

> *"There is nothing more elusive than an obvious fact."*

However, by investing the time to fully understand **who your audience is, the outcome you're trying to achieve, and the narrative that will tie it all together**, what you say will have the impact you want.

Specifically, it informs exactly *what* you're going to say, and *how* you're going to say it.

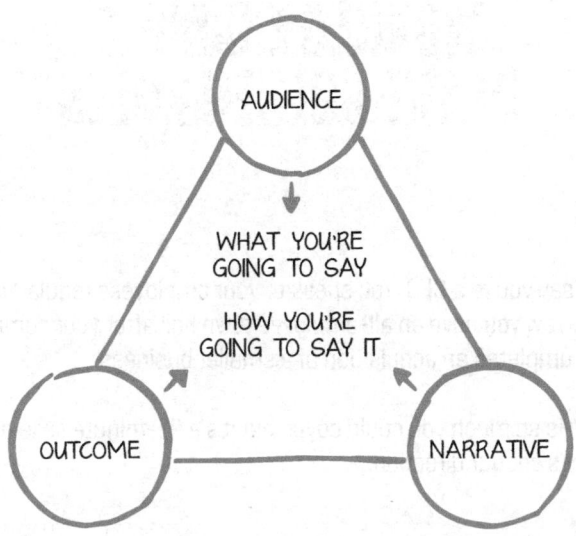

And it works uniformly.

No two presentations, speeches, podcasts, webinars, pitches or interviews are *ever* the same.

Ever.

This is why the Golden Rules are so important.

> **Whatever the scenario, they give you a familiar,
> cohesive and solid place to start.**

And they will set your direction.

Every time.

WORKED EXAMPLE OF THE GOLDEN RULES

Let's say you're a CEO. You speak to your employees regularly, but tomorrow you have an all-employee town hall after your company has completed an acquisition of a smaller business.

There is so much you could cover, but it's a 45-minute session. So, let's set our direction.

Who is your audience?
A combination of both people familiar with your business and those who are new, all still processing the news of what's happened with their companies.

What outcome are you trying to achieve?
You want to win hearts and minds, remove any uncertainty and doubt, and get the new teams collaborating quickly, effectively and profitably.

What is your narrative?
Turning the business logic for the merger into a clear rationale that relates to all employees about how this will benefit them as the business evolves.

By taking the time to apply the Golden Rules, you can form a very clear view of what you want to say, and how you're going to say it.

So, in this townhall scenario:

- The talk track will have to be clear, reasoned and easy to understand – not super-detailed and in the weeds.
  You'll want everyone to leave understanding exactly why this made sense.

- You'll want to take some time to introduce other speakers who need to be aligned with the messaging.
  Maybe even add a panel into part of it or possibly include a video montage of new leadership or something to break the ice.

- You'll probably want to be slide-light, with an open staging and not speaking behind a podium.
  The format will facilitate spending more time building a personal connection, including introducing yourself and other leaders to new employees.

- Your overall tone will need to be welcoming and encouraging with a good measure of enthusiasm so that people feel part of something exciting.
  This means avoiding too much corporate jargon.

- You will definitely want to anticipate some challenging questions.
  Some you'll want to address proactively, and then maybe leave more time for an open Q&A than a normal session.

- You'll want to end with clear takeaways and a timeline of what's expected of team members in the weeks and months to come.
  This way no one leaves the meeting feeling lost, confused, or uncertain about their role or future.

I don't claim that the above is an exhaustive list. But by applying the Golden Rules and using them to inform the content and delivery, you are immediately working with greater intent.

And while it might seem obvious, it never is –

- Speaking after a merger would be different than after an acquisition.

- Speaking at an annual meeting after a strong financial year is different from one focused on a company turnaround.

- A fundraiser following a leadership change is different from one following a major world event.

- A tech podcast with a panel of experts is different from an HR-focused podcast on your career story.

- A competitive pitch to a new client is different from re-pitching with an existing one.

- Media interviews for a big product launch are different from those following an investor day.

And if you're presenting as a team in some format, whether it's a company town hall or a new business pitch, *every* speaker needs to be aligned and focused on the same answers so that you're all working towards the same goals.

Simple.   Universal.   Effective.

Therefore, from this day forward, no matter what the scenario is or how long you've got to prepare, always take the time to determine your direction with intent by applying the Golden Rules and asking yourself:

Who is your audience?
What outcome are you trying to achieve?
What is your narrative?

SETTING DIRECTION:
INTENTIONALLY

Congratulations.

You now have the foundation to substantially improve your presentation and public speaking skills.

Simply put, taking time to apply and understand these Golden Rules before you do anything else will immediately improve your presentation because it will be deliberate and intentional.

Guaranteed.

And to be clear, I'm not suggesting this needs to be a long, convoluted process. Far from it.

But it *is* a necessary process.

From wedding toast to fundraising speech, from economics podcast to company general meeting, the Golden Rules will always set your direction.

That means you're guaranteed to not only have greater command of how you speak and the message you want to deliver, but you'll have greater command of the outcome you want to achieve.

Every time.

Let's not be complacent, we're only at the beginning, *but at least we know where we're going.*

There are a lot more skills that can and should be applied to amplify what you have to say.

That's what the rest of this book is here to show you.

But while the rest of the book will now be more focused on the practical execution of building and delivering your content, they all tie back to everything in this chapter.

> **Every time you are going to speak,**
> **come back to these Golden Rules so you**
> **accurately and effectively set the direction**
> **for WHAT you deliver and HOW you deliver it.**

Now, let's set the direction for utter brilliance.

BUILDING YOUR CONTENT

Good presentation is never style over substance. Never.

While there are sections in this book that will talk about the delivery of your speech, pitch or presentation, this is arguably the most important chapter.

Developing, structuring and ordering your content effectively is critical – whatever the scenario.

It puts the Golden Rules in context and forms the bedrock of what you go on to deliver verbally.

In this chapter, we go through how to build your talk track and presentation materials so that at every stage, from initial brainstorming to final edit, you're doing so in service of the Golden Rules.

And in doing so, this section will provide the tools to level the playing field.

The beauty of a somewhat structured and easy-to-apply approach is that it is exactly that.

Whether you have months to plan for a main-stage keynote, or just minutes to prepare for a last-minute addition to a team meeting, this section will get you there.

And it will get you there while ensuring impact and persuasion.

So, as we approach this chapter, think of it as a blueprint. And in time, the process will become second nature.

1. **Three is a magic number**; organize your content for optimal impact.
2. **Take a tip from stand-up**; use primacy and recency to focus attention.
3. **Slides are not the presentation**; you are.

JUST LIKE A JIGSAW PUZZLE, START WITH THE CORNERS

You've been asked to speak on a topic.

I'm delighted for you.

Now step away from the PowerPoint deck.
Go on, back a bit more.
Further.

Because if you're applying the Golden Rules fully, you'll be creating something very specific to the scenario.

So, first you need to find the shape and the parameters.

That means before you create anything, you need to write down a list of the ideas, themes, topics, examples you *may* want to include.

Kind of like tipping all the jigsaw pieces out so you can start to find the corners and the edges to anchor the picture you're going to build.

And yes, you read that correctly: write, not type.

I'm adamant about this and not because I'm old fashioned.

There are numerous and repeated studies that have shown that engaging the fine motor system to produce letters and words by hand has a strong positive effect on learning and memory.

So even though this is nowhere near your final presentation, you're already ingraining it.*

Then, and only then, when you have amassed a collection of the thoughts and ideas needed to meet the Golden Rules – *audience, outcome, narrative* – can you start to bring those thoughts into an actual presentation.

*I also recommend writing your final speech notes (which we'll get to) by hand for this very reason.

THREE *IS* A MAGIC NUMBER

What do Steve Jobs, the Marine Corps, and Rice Crispies all have in common?

All of them are examples of how the rule of three generates impact and aids memory retention.

Omne trium perfectum ['*the rule of three*' in Latin, not a Hogwarts' spell] is an established principle that leverages our psychological ability to recognize and remember patterns.

For centuries it has been used in business, marketing and public speaking to provide structure, aid recall and prevent the listener/consumer being overwhelmed.

How did Caesar describe how he won the war?
"*I came, I saw, I conquered.*"

How did Steve Jobs describe the iPad2?
"*Thinner, lighter, faster.*"

And the Marine Corps considers the rule of three a matter of both pride and safety. Limiting a marine's attention to three tasks or goals, infinite possibilities are distilled to three distinct courses of action, avoiding confusion or being overwhelmed.

It's an *exceptionally* powerful tool. And now that you know about it, I guarantee you'll see it everywhere.

Do this simple exercise every time:
- Take the talking points you've sketched out,
- Identify where similar themes develop in a larger narrative, and
- See how you can arrange the talking points into three distinct groups.

Remember also that the three pillars don't need to be equal. Some may be short, impactful ideas and some may be more nuanced. This is about organizing, not weighting.

And it doesn't have to be complicated:

Business progress to date, plans for current fiscal year, long-term goals

or

Macro-economic impacts, political dynamics, industry challenges and opportunities

The process is also a great editing tool when you have too many ideas to put together. Got an idea or concept that's an outlier? Ask yourself: can it be incorporated with another group if framed differently? If not, then let it go.

I promise that in doing so, it will not only help you order your thoughts, but lead you to a delivery of material that, when presented, will be *much* more impactful to your listener.

Now, go group your content in a form that will snap, crackle and pop!

A NOTE ON
THE RULE OF THREE

I promise I'll only do this once.

The rule of three concept is the one that I most often get pushback on in one of two ways, so I'm heading the detractors off at the pass.

1. *"But I'm covering our company's five-point plan; I can't leave two out."*

   I'm not asking you to, and you've missed the point.

   And it ignores the second Golden Rule: *why* are you talking about the plan in the first place?

   Instead, maybe you need to structure the five-point plan in terms of:
   › *The market landscape and need for a new plan,*
   › *How the plan is structured and designed, and*
   › *How you want people to apply it.*

2. *"I did the exercise and there are definitely four topics that we need to cover."*

   All good. Cover all four.

Remember this whole book is a set of guidelines, not train tracks.

The idea of this book is to make you think and help perfect your approach.

The very fact that you went through the exercise and structured your talking points into distinct topics has already made your presentation more cohesive and compelling.

THE CARDINAL RULE OF ORDINAL POINTS

Now you have three distinct themes or sections of content, you need to organize them in order of impact.

This means understanding which is the strongest of the three points and starting from there.

The easiest way for me to explain why this is important is going back to my roots as a courtroom lawyer, where everything is an act of persuasion.

There is a temptation to save the strongest point for last, so you finish with impact, starting with points that are only so-so, rather than capturing their attention from the get-go. Far from a big reveal, burying the lead ends up creating an unnecessary uphill struggle for yourself.

However, if you start with the strongest, most convincing point, the chances of having the tribunal on your side is heightened. You're starting from a position of strength, delivering your strongest point when they're most attentive. This in turn positions points two and three as further support of the overall argument, which the tribunal is already somewhat persuaded by.

This principle applies with all presentations.

Because remember our Golden Rules: we're trying to lead a specific audience to an irresistible outcome set in a narrative that is clear and makes sense.

This means ordering your themes or sections in the order of importance to your audience.

> Take an annual meeting where you want to satisfy investors and have them support your plan:
> - Business progress to date (shows business is secure),
> - plans for the current fiscal year (shows profitable plan now it's secure),
> - long-term goals (opportunities if it goes well).

The power it gives and the ease in which it guides message delivery is worth its weight in gold. Especially if they are key decision makers.

Say you've got 15 minutes to pitch changing your advertising platform to your CEO, who is highly competitive and wants to make sure the company is *always* using the most technology.

You're not going to *start* with potential cost savings if what you're proposing is the most advanced tech that no one else has. Cost is important, but it could come across as penny pinching if that's how you start. Instead, you want to get them excited about it being *avant-garde*, having a competitive advantage, and then guess what … we'll also save money. Win-win.

COLOURING INSIDE
THE LINES

You've almost got your content complete: just two more steps.

One thing a presentation is not is a list of statements.

Tailoring your content to your specific audience in a compelling and persuasive way requires taking the list of messages/topics you have to deliver and then bringing them to life.

Luckily, there are a set of content 'paints' – or proof points – you can lift off your easel.

Personal experience
A short story, anecdote or example that you can use to bring your key points to life in some way:
"Mentoring needs to be central to our HR plan. I think of my own career, and how my very first boss taught me a guiding principle I still apply to this day, which is ..."

Primary facts/stats
Stats or data points that you or your organization owns that gives evidence to an issue or a challenge – especially if it's visual:
"When we looked at the data, we saw that footfall to our museum halved within the first week of the building work taking place, and as the works became delayed so did ..."

Secondary data
Tests, trials or surveys that give comparable data:
"Oxbridge University published a study in 2023 that showed this phenomenon is already occurring in other sectors, and predicts it will in ours if these changes aren't made ..."

Analogies
Comparison or contrast that likens the idea you're trying to convey into a recognizable or real-world scenario:
"You know the story about two hikers being chased by a bear and one stops to put his sneakers on? We can't outrun everything, but we can outrun the competition ..."

Customer examples
Real-world decision-making impacted by choices or actions:
"Last week I asked a FoodMart customer what they liked about our new store layout, and without hesitating she said ..."

To be persuasive, each of your three themes will need a combination of these to bring them to life.

Begin by deciding the most salient points in each theme and see which of these can effectively add colour to the picture you're trying to paint.

Do so, and you'll be sure to colour me impressed.

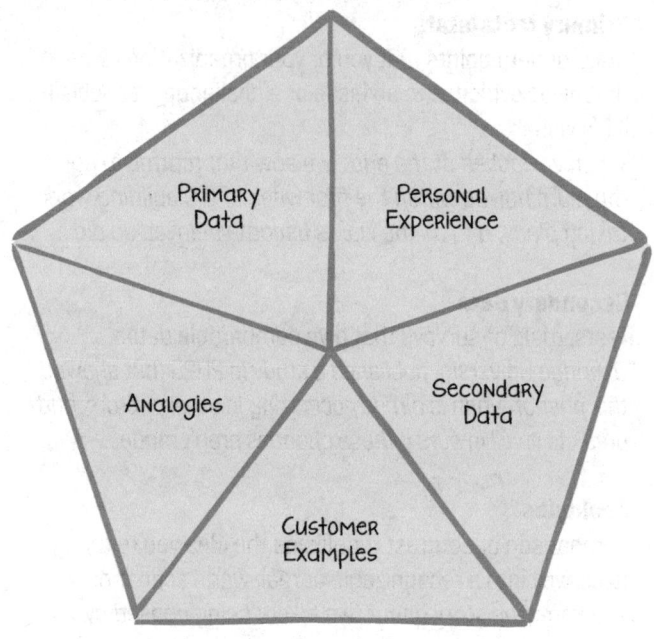

STAND UP FOR YOUR FINAL BOW

By now you should be pretty close to the final content outline you're either going to speak to or build slides for.

Either way, there is a final step based on a psychological trick that is incredibly powerful.

It's such an established concept that stand-up comedians use it almost without exception.

And that's the primacy and recency effect, which means people generally remember – and are emotionally impacted by – that which they experienced first and last.

Most stand-up comics will say they use this technique, always starting their set with their strongest joke and ending with their second best.

Why? Because if you grab the audience's attention and knock their socks off as soon as you start and then walk off the stage leaving them howling with laughter, this will shape their experience of the whole set.

So now you have the body of your presentation, you need to package it up:

> *How will you open so that you grab your audience's attention?*
> and
> *How will you close leaving them compelled to pursue
> a call to action?*

And providing the opening and closing connect with each other and the overarching theme/topic – all feeding into the Golden Rules – the world is your lobster.

- It could be an impactful statistic that makes the presentation relevant or timely,

- It could be a heartfelt or funny personal anecdote that brings a revelation or a surprise,

- It could be a famous quote that connects you with the audience,

- It could be a video of a real-life example of themes you've been talking about, or

- It could be a rhetorical question, the answer being the action you're trying to bring about.

This is not exhaustive. Every presentation is different; there is no one-size-fits-all answer to this.

But let me leave you with this as a call to action:

If you can increase the impact and persuasiveness of your entire presentation by simply adding a bold idea with conviction to start and the close – why wouldn't you?

PLACING YOUR SANDWICH ORDER TO GO

OK, so you've followed the process – you're almost there.

By now you should have the following:

Opening
- quote, statistic, anecdote, customer example, etc. to grab attention

Key Topic One
- your most persuasive theme/topic, supported with proof points

Key Topic Two
- your next most persuasive theme/topic, supported with proof points

Key Topic Three
- your final persuasive theme/topic, supported with proof points

Closing
- powerful and memorable close with clear call to action for audience

---

That's it.

The framework for a clear and compelling presentation is no more complicated than that.

It's like a really good sandwich: bread on either side, and enough filling and flavour to be tasty, without being overwhelming. Kind of like a great BLT.

The beauty of it is, it gives you the discipline to build your content for something you have time to plan – be it a wedding toast or a main-stage keynote conversation.

But it also gives you the structure if you have to do something on the fly.

If the CEO or chairperson of the board said to you, right now, *"I know it wasn't on the agenda, but can you give a quick update on initiative X after the coffee break?"* you could.

Because this structure not only orders your thoughts (and makes them easy to digest for your listeners), but helps you deliver against the Golden Rules by turning your ideas into a compelling presentation.

This is a big step. This is probably the biggest unlock in this whole book.

I'm proud of you.
Now go grab a BLT. You earned it.

WORKED EXAMPLE OF CONTENT BUILDING

Even though we've gone step by step, it's probably worth doing a worked example.

You're the CEO of a medical technology company, and you've been invited to speak at an industry conference about the evolution of tech in the healthcare industry.

First, the Golden Rules:
Who is your audience?
Medical professionals who are highly engaged and knowledgeable

What outcome are you trying to achieve?
Raise awareness and use by medical practitioners of a recently developed technology your company has created

What is your narrative?
Your company has been – and continues to be – the leading innovator in this field, with a track record of improving patient outcomes

It's very simple. But you can see how – in just a short page – you've now very clearly outlined exactly what your talk track is and how it all fits together.

Your content then could build in the following:

Opener

Big, surprising statistic on how much treatment due to late diagnosis costs hospitals annually, contextualized as a percentage of annual budget

Key Topic One

This continues to be one of the highest misdiagnosed areas in the field

- Secondary data from healthcare providers on macro trends of illness
- Primary data from your market research when developing product on why this is

Key Topic Two

The cost of treatment for this area is skyrocketing

- Secondary data from hospital trust on wait times and impact to care
- Customer survey on how many people are concerned about potential cost

Key Topic Three

Early diagnosis is where there should be focus

- Analogy with similar medical innovation and data on patient outcomes
- Medical example of where your technology was a success

Close

Personal experience of how one of your family was impacted, how it is a driver of your company mission and personal motivation for audience to prevent it happening to others

SPECIAL MENTION:
CONTENT FOR PITCHES

I do want to take a moment to double-click on content development if you're pitching competitively for something like an investment or to win a contract.

The stakes are higher because you're asking for money. Persuading someone into a buying decision, especially in a business environment, therefore needs a greater level of influence.

The most effective way to achieve it is ensuring you have *benefit-led messaging*.

While this could take a book in its own right, too many people focus on the features of their product or their work, and not the advantages or benefits they bring that make it irresistible.

Good messaging gets the features and advantages, but *great and persuasive messaging* articulates the benefits clearly to the person making the decision ... so they *have* to have it.

FAB components:

> **Features** are factual descriptions of a product's characteristics:
> *An AI-driven tool that organizes and de-dupes your business invoices and receipts*

Advantages describe how these features are beneficial:
Automating all your accounting processes, therefore reducing time and cost by 75%

Benefits explain the positive outcomes that the customer experiences as a result:
Increasing your profitabilty so you can grow your business faster

The easiest way to understand it is the following exercise. Simply write down and prioritize the answers to the following question:

If I took price out of the equation, what can the buyer do/ achieve with what I'm offering that no one else can offer?

Because if you can quickly get to the benefit part of your messaging, you'll unlock the eureka moment that makes your proposition irresistible.

"Wait, that's what I'll be able to achieve/that's the opportunity? Sign me up!"

It's a valuable discipline to master.

It's highly effective in pitching and sales, and works for any product, any service, any offering ... even book titles ... because you want to be utterly brilliant, don't you?

SPECIAL MENTION:
CONTENT FOR C-SUITE LEADERS

A specific piece of advice for C-suite leaders is that when speaking specifically to stakeholders who are emotionally or monetarily invested in your brand (employees, investors, customers), consistency is a critical element of building the necessary trust needed to be persuasive.

However, bringing consistency to the forefront of your narrative can be tricky.

It must be tangible and demonstrable consistency. Because people will immediately see through simple repetition, presenteeism or tubthumping; then you're in negative trust territory.

Happily, there is a simple effective approach: applying the 'SAY:DO' ratio.

Simply put, repeatedly using the same clear and consistent language for the things you promise to do, and then clearly stating that you've delivered on them:

"At the start of the year we promised to double our profitability. We're now six months in and I'm happy to report we're comfortably tracking ahead of target."

"Last quarter you'll remember we promised to invest more in employee benefits, so today I'm happy to announce the launch of ..."

And this is especially impactful if you repeat the same specific language – like an 'efficiency programme' or 'innovation roadmap' – because it aids recall while demonstrating reliability.

It becomes iterative and especially relevant for things like employee town halls and earnings calls.

It also means your other C-suite team can refer to it and know that other team members immediately think of the broader concept.

High SAY:DO = High Trust

I particularly advocate this concept for CEOs because it's also helpful in maintaining trust if there is a miss, because you're transparent while also providing the mechanism to explain how you're proactively solving for it.

> *"In Q1, we set out our plan for $10 million of savings. At the midpoint, the broader economic conditions mean we're slightly behind where we'd like to be and so I'll spend the rest of our time outlining in detail how we're stepping up the plan, so we still meet our goal."*

A simple yet *highly* effective technique.

THE FINAL STEP:
ANTICIPATING QUESTIONS

It's also important to note that good presentation skills involve seeing around corners.

A vital part of planning your content also means planning for questions.

Taking time to think about what questions your audience might ask – especially the tricky ones or those you'd prefer not to answer – and pre-empting them is important for two reasons:

First, it makes you look prepared and instils confidence. Plain and simple.

Any audience will be impressed if you've already thought about their question, anticipated it, considered it and have a meaningful answer for it.

Second, if you plan it in advance – either by adding it proactively into your talk track *or* cementing the response should you be asked – you control the narrative.

You won't be thrown off your game, because you're not surprised. And you'll also have thought carefully about the answer you would *want* to give, not the quick knee-jerk response that might not be as compelling.

Imagine you're pitching a big project idea. As you finalize your content, you need to do the following exercise:

Write down the five toughest questions you're likely to get on this and then check:
- Is there any value in adding the answer *proactively* into my talk track
  - › Look back over materials and see where you can address it
- Is this something I'd prefer *not* to raise proactively?
  - › Then make sure you have a robust answer if asked

Examples:
What's this project going to cost?
- This question is going to come up, you know the answer, and you want to be able to respond by focusing on the ROI – *go back and see where it fits into the talk track.*

What happens if there is a delay in implementation?
- You probably *don't* want to be emphasizing the downsides in your presentation but it's a valid question – *prepare the question with a strong answer of how you'll mitigate.*

PLAN ON A PAGE

At this point, I'm often asked if there is a template for a content framework.

Here's what I'd recommend but put it in a format that works best for you.

Opening: Statement/Quote/Statistic/Idea		
Key Topic One	**Key Topic Two**	**Key Topic Three**
Talking point ▪ Proof point Talking point ▪ Proof point Talking point ▪ Proof point	Talking point ▪ Proof point Talking point ▪ Proof point Talking point ▪ Proof point	Talking point ▪ Proof point Talking point ▪ Proof point Talking point ▪ Proof point
Closing: Impactful call to action		

Q & A	
Question One	Answer (proof point if needed)
Question Two	Answer (proof point if needed)
Question Three	Answer (proof point if needed)
Question Four	Answer (proof point if needed)
Question Five	Answer (proof point if needed)

SLIDEY SLOPE

Slides.
Slides, slides, slides ...

There are days that I cheer for PowerPoint and Keynote and all the rest.
There are other days when I curse them.

They are a fantastic tool. They really are.

But the majority of presentations that lack impact do so because the slides and the materials have taken over.

They become overwhelming to the audience and the presenter becomes a slave to them.

And it's probably because they were the first thing to be created, and then the talk track built around it. This becomes a slippery slope, because more and more information gets added to the slides – for fear of missing something out on the slide itself – and it pulls all the focus.

If the first half of this chapter hasn't shown why this approach just doesn't create the most impactful content, then something is amiss.

But there is something I want to instil in everyone's psyche right here, right now:

The slides are NOT the presentation. YOU are.
I'll repeat.

The slides are NOT the presentation. YOU are.

Slides are nothing more than ONE tool to bring your talk track and your ideas to life.

You do not need a slide for every idea you present.

You do not need every slide to include your ideas verbatim in text.

You do not need the slides as a crutch.

If you have prepared well, I'll be so bold as to say that you do not *need* the slides AT ALL.

Please make this your first, your enduring and your last thought as you build your presentation materials.

If you can get that truly ingrained in your approach to presentations and your delivery technique, then your presenting and public speaking abilities will truly excel.

FREE PARKING 24/7

When you come to build your slide deck, the first thing you should do, the *very* first, is put a 'parking lot' at the back.

And most important of all, while you're building your deck, don't delete anything.

Anything.

Chances are the idea was probably inspired by something and will come in useful somehow.

So, use a parking lot.

Any slides that don't quite fit, or any ideas you have but are not sure where to put, park them.

Why?

Because that way no work is wasted and nothing is lost.

Because that way you don't need to suffer through version control hell to find it again.

Because if you do want to put the idea back, it's far quicker to edit than recreate afresh.

Because when one of your bosses inevitably says, "Do we have anything on ..." or "Do we have a different version of ..." you can just zip to the back.

And because that way you keep your main presentation tidy, and you won't pave paradise to put up a ... never mind.

SLIDING SCALE

Before you start you also need to think about how much content you're going to build so you can balance it out – I'll keep this one short – keep your slide deck short.

I have lost count of how many times I've seen people build a 30-slide deck for a 30-minute presentation.

That equates to one slide a minute *if* you start on time, don't do intros and don't take questions.

Which means you're just going to be racing through it all.

But it's a presentation, not clay pigeon shooting.

PULL!!

No.

Pull back.

My personal rule of thumb is MAX one slide per five minutes (unless say you have a couple of slides that are just images you want to flick through, which is reasonable).

And then make sure you have some time at the beginning and end for intros and questions.

Do that maths:

$$\frac{30 \text{ minutes presentation - 5 mins for questions}}{5 \text{ minutes per slide}} = 5 \text{ slides}$$

I know this is going to cause UTTER consternation.

I can literally hear the pearls being clutched and the intake of breath.

But you need to remember two things:
1. The slides are NOT the presentation. <u>YOU are.</u>
2. Think of your audience. Bombarding them with slides is overwhelming. That's not what you're here to do; you're here to persuade them.

Pull back.
And give you and your content room to be absorbed.

PRIORITIZING VISUALIZING

You've decided some slides will be useful, you have opened a new file, and you've put a parking lot at the back.

There is a temptation to start typing.

However, if you're applying the Golden Rules – and how you make your content persuasive to *this specific* audience – you should really be asking yourself:

> *How do I bring my ideas to life visually?*

NOT

> *How do I summarize this idea in words?*

This is a discipline that I believe too many people have forgotten. Which is why people just start typing.

Stop.

The purpose of the slide is to help *visualize* the talk track or concepts you're delivering.

This means that for each concept that requires a slide, first think if you can increase the persuasive effect of what you're trying to convey with one of the following:

Image	Process flow
Diagram	Organizational chart
Graphs/chart	Decision tree
Infographic	Quote

These are the things that slides are designed for, and these are the things that will add impact or clarity to the ideas you're putting forward.

Of course, they don't work for everything, but they *should* be your starting point.

And that doesn't mean you can put lots of words just in a pretty format. Oh no, no, no ...

PRESENTING, NOT WORD SEARCHING

The overuse of slides in meetings has also led to an epidemic of people not editing the content they put on their slides.

Even if you understand that slides are about visual representation of an idea, people often still think that *every* thought and idea needs to go onto the slide.

If so, why are you speaking? Send an email.

The more words you have on a slide, the more your audience will be reading what's on the screen, not what you're saying.

Being ruthless with your slides means the spotlight swings back to you.

But if text *is* critical you need to include it meaningfully.

Fortunately, there *is* a formula to help.

THE 5-5-5 FORMULA

At this point you'll probably realize I have some strong opinions about slides.

You're correct.

But rather than just tell you what not to do, I'm here to give advice.

While there are a number of 'rules' about slides, there is one formula that I think is most helpful, and that's the 5-5-5 formula for using text on slides.

I will admit that this takes a little time.

But the time you spend focusing on the text edits is worth it. Because it means your audience will spend more time focusing on you.

I can't help but think of Mark Twain every time I see a slide chock-a-block with text.

> *"I didn't have time to write a short letter, so I wrote a long one instead."*

Slides are no different: clear and to the point will *always* be clear and to the point.

Avoid more than **five words** on a single line
- Limiting the number of words makes it easier to digest for the audience, and they can also glance at it rather than read it when they're supposed to be listening to you.
- *Path to bonus accretion in fiscal 2024* becomes *FY24 Bonus Strategy*

Avoid more than **five lines** of text on a single slide
- Blocks of text create brain drain, and it's hard for your audience to locate the idea you're speaking to. It also means there's no room for diagrams or illustrations to bring it to life.

Avoid more than **five slides** of text in a row
- And because variety is the spice of life, text after text is too much. You need to break it up with images, diagrams or anything you can to keep the content balanced, engaging and informative.

SLIDE CHECKPOINT

OK, time for a quick sense check.

Step one: Volume	Time: slides ≤ 1 slide : every 5 minutes Too many? - move to the parking lot - consolidate
Step two: Visualize	Review each slide: Could this be visualized rather than plain text? Yes – replace/redesign No – proceed to step three
Step three: Verbiage	Apply the 5-5-5 formula Max 5 words to a line Max 5 lines to a slide Max 5 slides of text in a row

There's an easy way to rember this:

Making sure you check the three Vs - volume, vizualize, and verbage - you will be certain to give your slide deck Va Va Voom!

A NOTE ON DESIGNERS

If you can, *please* use a designer – or someone with strong presentation software skills – to do the final sweep of your presentation.

Nothing is more jarring than inconsistent colours, odd fonts, different sizes, things not aligned.

Again, I may seem like I'm focused on something trivial, but it really isn't.

It's the slide equivalent to cleaning your shoes, brushing your teeth and showing up on time.

Think of it this way:

> *If you can't take the time to ensure your materials are tidy, accurate and well presented, why should your audience take the time?*

Take the time at the final hurdle to get some design input.

And then, MUCH more important than that:

LEAVE IT ALONE!!

Especially if you have an inhouse design team that knows your organization's design standards.

Trust them. They know what they're doing.

I've been lucky enough to work with many creative teams and designers. The collective sigh that goes up when slides appear that you've 'redesigned' late at night after the design team sent them is NOT a sound you want to hear.

> I genuinely once saw a design team spend *days* on a presentation that looked *stunning*, only for the lawyer who asked for it to be done to put screenshots of a Microsoft Word version he designed himself … yes you read that right … on the main stage because he didn't like the photos anymore. Don't be that person.

Need a change? Ask them, and in good time.

Please.

CONSISTENCY IMPROVES CLARITY

Copyediting is a vital part of communication but often gets forgotten with slides.

Because your slides contain short and impactful ideas (because you deleted all those long sentences, didn't you?), then you need a good copyedit for consistency.

If you're referring to something as a 'strategy', then keep referring to it that way.

'Phases 1, 2 and 3,' or what have you, should be clear and easy to discern.

Names of people should be spelled exactly.

Numbers should follow a consistent decimalization or rounding up.

Icons or logos should be correct, up to date and consistent.

You get the point.

It's important because if you're doing it right, then the slides should be creating the visual memory for your audience along with your talk track.

Mistakes and inconsistencies will get in the way of the message you're trying to deliver.

Because for audiences they're easy to spot. And they'll trip you up, so they won't resonate.

It's also *super* important to remember that slides are often shared among teams or used to guide meetings if information is being cascaded down teams. Therefore, consistency is even more vital to prevent accidental misinterpretation or confusion.

Therefore, be ruthless with yourself when you edit.

Personally, I *always* do a printed version so I can do a slide-by-side-by-slide comparison; even better if you do multiple slides to a page (because that can be a helpful prompt sheet as you're reviewing).

And if you can, ask someone to look over your slides for you. They're almost guaranteed to spot something you haven't seen.

Your materials will be all the more impactful for it.

SLIDE DELIVERY 1:
BRING THE SCREEN TO LIFE

As we close on slides, I want to give three quick notes about presentation delivery when using slides, which, although they sort of belong in the next chapter, are helpful to understand as you're building your deck.

The first is the most important, and that's to think like a weather forecaster.
And no, I don't mean keeping an eye out for areas of high pressure.

TV weather forecasters balance what you're seeing on the screen with what they're describing to you, in turn drawing your attention to the most salient points. There is a synergy, but they are also in the driving seat.

Your relationship with slides should be the same.

> Whether the slides have a visualization of some sort, or are text based, you need to ask yourself:
>
> *What am I saying about this slide to demonstrate its importance or relevance when it is on the screen?*

If you're simply going to be repeating what's written on the slide – the slide isn't right if the slide speaks for itself without you adding anything. You're not doing it right.

It's an important step because everything has to be additive to the overall narrative.

Got a slide with an important graph that is analogous to your business case?
How are you going to set up the slide? What part of the graph do you want them to focus on? How are you going to demonstrate the relevance?

Got a slide with an image on it?
What is the context of the image? What is it you see that you want them to think about?

Doing this will not only ground and enhance the strength of your presentation, but it will connect the visual narrative with the verbal narrative to increase the persuasiveness.

Just let the slide hang there, and you'll be lingering in the doldrums.

SLIDE DELIVERY 2:
AGENDA SETTING

An agenda slide at the beginning of a presentation is *always* helpful, even if brief.

It gives your audience a quick overview of what you're going to be covering, allows them to start focusing on what questions they might ask, and also gives an indication of how long you are going to be speaking.

It will also help ground your presentation with something you know well, allowing you to speak with a strong start.

But **please** don't read the whole agenda out and then summarize everything you're going to cover before you cover it. That becomes terribly repetitive and boring.

Instead, show the slide, give an indication of how long you'll be covering the topics, and then the magic component: begin the act of persuasion.

> *"Today we're going to be covering the latest stage of our product developments and where we've made great progress, so we can then focus on why we think further investment will bring a really strong ROI."*

Or

"This afternoon I'm going to touch on the key stages of this new proposed housing development and then spend time hearing from you on how we can also make it beneficial to the community."

This does two important things:
1. It signals to your audience you have done your homework and are well prepared (and not just reading at them), and

2. It frames the whole presentation for the listener with the ask you're going to make of them. It gets both their and your brain in gear.

This way, you plant the seeds of persuasion before you even start the presentation and set the path for an *irresistible* outcome.

SLIDE DELIVERY 3:
SLIDE DRAIN = BRAIN DRAIN

Finally, I have to air the pet peeve of *every* human being I know. And that is witnessing the following from a speaker:

"Now I'm not going to drain the slide, but ..."

speaker reads every sentence on slide and also gives additional context

Ten minutes later:

"Now let's move ahead as I know we're short on time."

CLICK

speaker reads every sentence on slide and also gives additional context

Ten minutes later:

> (repeat *ad nauseum*)

Consider this a public service announcement.

Never do this. Ever.

CLICK

BUILDING YOUR CONTENT
- CLOSING THOUGHTS

If this chapter has done anything, I hope it's quashed the mistaken belief that being a good public speaker is something that just comes naturally.

Sure, some people find it easier. And yes, there are techniques that can significantly elevate message delivery, much of which we'll cover in the next chapter.

> **But fundamentally, compelling and persuasive public speaking in any form comes from a foundation of clear and structured content tailored specifically to the audience and the outcome you want to achieve.**

If the Golden Rules set the direction, then content structure is the vehicle to get you there.

Building and structuring the content is 90% of the work; the rest is delivery.

The beauty is that taking a disciplined approach makes everything else easier *and* more impactful.

It's like those actors, models or singers that you see walking down the street looking effortlessly cool. The reality is that a lot of behind-the-scenes thought, and work, went into that crafting that impacts you in a single moment.

There is, in fact, a word for this: *sprezzatura*.

As defined by the author Baldassare Castiglione, sprezzatura is a kind of effortless grace, defined particularly by the art of remaining nonchalant while making something difficult or complex look easy.

I think this is what people mean when they refer to a brilliant public speaker as 'a natural.'

Most of the hard work happened before the speaker even stepped on the stage.

Which means you now have the foundation to be utterly brilliant also.

DELIVERING WITH IMPACT

By now you should have a firm idea of what you're going to say.

Now it's about how you elevate the delivery of it.

I'm going to rip the band-aid off first. While there *is* a formula for how you build the content you're going to present, there *isn't* a formula for how you deliver it in each scenario.

Conversations and human interactions don't work like that.

But before you go slamming the book closed and dashing for a refund, it's important to stress that this book is a guide to improve your public speaking, not to strip you of your authenticity.

The world would be terribly dull, and it would be very hard to be compelling and stand out from the crowd, if we all spoke the same.

Authenticity matters.

And as I said before, good public speaking and presenting are never about style over substance.

But there are still skills that can be learned and applied to really elevate your message delivery.

So, this chapter is dedicated to how you command your audiences' attention and leave a lasting impression through authentic and compelling delivery.

1. **Light the fire**, prepare yourself, bring enthusiasm, harness nerves.
2. **Set the course for space flight**, use your words, voice and posture for maximum impact.
3. **Rehearse your way**, but always from pillar to post.

LIGHT THE FIRE

There are a lot of techniques and guidance in this book, all of which can be applied and adjusted.

At the highest level, though, the combination of preparation, enthusiasm and nerves is always key to igniting excellent message delivery.

The easiest way to think of it is the three things a fire needs: fuel, heat and oxygen

Or in our terms:

Fuel – Everything gathered and prepared for delivery

Heat – Conviction in what you're saying to inspire others

Oxygen – Harnessing your nerves to propel you throughout

I won't claim everything else is just polishing.

Far from it.

But it's a good place to start.

After that, you can layer on the use of words, voice and physicality to further enhance your delivery, enhancing your persuasiveness throughout.

FUEL:
PREPARATION

This may seem painfully obvious, but I'm not just talking about preparing your talk track.

You have to thoroughly gather and prepare your materials, and you have to rehearse.

But what I'm talking about is more fundamental.

I'm talking about getting yourself in a prepared state *to* speak. Because you can't start a fire with soggy twigs.

In practical terms, this means doing everything you can to set yourself up for success and to remove everything out of your way that will be a detractor.

Planning ahead, so you're not arriving at the last minute in a fluster.

Reading around your subject or studying the bios of attendees.

Checking out the venue beforehand, walking the stage, checking the room layout.

Making sure you have your slides and notes saved, and your laptop charged.

This is what gives you fuel ready for success.

Like my grandfather (a navy pilot) used to tell me:

> *"Even the most seasoned pilots do a pre-flight check
> before every take-off."*

Do your homework and do everything you can to avoid surprises.

Because surprises will throw you off your game, you want
to build on all the work you've done leading up to this point,
not have it evaporate.

And effective, influential and inspiring message delivery requires
a sure footing.

Think about the level of focus top athletes have on their face
before they run, jump, somersault.

THAT.

That is the level of focus and preparation you're aiming for.

This is the most important preparation you can do because it
gives you everything you need to perform at your best.

HEAT:
ENTHUSIASM

By enthusiasm, I don't mean energy. There is a note on that later.

I'm talking about genuinely conveying the interest, belief and enthusiasm for the subject you're presenting.

Let me ask you: have you ever been to a restaurant and one of the team asks if you'd like to hear the specials,' only to give a list of things in such a disinterested manner that they sound less special than the regular menu?

That is what I'm talking about with enthusiasm. Because if they're not persuaded by it, why would you be?

Simply put, if you don't deliver what you have to say with the passion and drive to convey, it's just words.

Enthusiasm comes from really engaging in the topic you're talking about.

Sometimes it's hard. Sometimes it's early or late or you don't have the motivation yourself to deliver on a topic.

Dig deep and bring it out.

Because enthusiasm is infectious, it really is.

Actors do it every day. Musicians do it every day. Newscasters do it every day.

And if you're finding it really hard to muster, check whether there is something about the content or the format that you're working with that is getting in the way.

Am I missing something that will really bring this to life?

Then deliver in a way that clearly demonstrates your enthusiasm for the topic.

Because if your heart isn't in it, then the audience's won't be either.

OXYGEN:
NERVES

The final ingredient is understanding and accepting that nerves are normal.

Always.

Every time.

Experience doesn't negate nerves. Public speaking in any form is a responsibility.

And it's a new responsibility every time you do it.

Make your peace with it.

Instead apply the Einsteinian law of thermodynamics: energy can't be created or destroyed but it can be transformed.

The increase in your heart rate and sweaty palms are not indicative that you won't be able to speak well.

Nerves can become adrenaline.

Adrenaline gives you focus.

So, accept that nerves are normal.

Don't try to hush them: harness them.

FLIGHT TO SPACEFLIGHT

These three things – heat, fuel and oxygen – will give you the things you need for your presentation technique to take flight.

If you grasp those things alone, your technique and ability will instantly improve.

Guaranteed.

Winning and focused delivery comes from a winning and focused mindset.

They are simple, they are easy to apply, and they work together.

But I want you to be *utterly* brilliant.

Flight is good. I'm here to help you achieve space flight!

Importantly, obtaining space flight takes more training and has more variables.

That's OK. *This* is your inflight manual.

But start applying these techniques one by one in ways that resonate with you, and you'll be shooting for the stars in no time.

ENERGY = IMPACT²

Don't worry, I'm not going to waffle on any more about laws of thermodynamics.

But it's important upfront to understand that the energy you bring to a speaking engagement can have an outsized impact on your audience.

Calm, quiet energy can make your audience lean in more and creates suspense.

Measured energy and a steady voice can instil confidence and convey control.

Lively and fun energy can convey personal enthusiasm or stir up a crowd.

You need to think about the dynamic *you* bring to the stage, and the emotional reaction you want to have.

It reminds me of a teacher at 6th form college, the late Dr David Pook, who had to teach Old Testament Bible studies between 2.30 and 4.30 on a Friday afternoon: 'the graveyard slot.'

But, knowing that, teaching this topic last class on a Friday to sleepy teenagers made him over-index on the humour, the energy and our participation. Now, almost 30 years on, I still remember substantially more from this class than any other.

Remember, communication is an audience-defined action.

The energy that you bring matters.

And there needs to be balance.

Just because it's interesting or exciting doesn't mean you need to be shouty all the way through.

Even action films have calm moments; otherwise, it becomes overwhelming.

Take time to understand the high points, the low points, the moments for consideration, the moments for excitement and convey it to your audience.

So, whether it's for the whole session or specific parts, think about how you can amplify your impact with the energy you bring.

CLIMB EVERY (STORY) MOUNTAIN

Because we've talked a lot about anecdotes and personal experiences being used as proof points, it's important to understand the vital skill of verbal storytelling.

And all compelling stories have a cadence and a flow that brings them to life and makes them compelling to listen to.

Bringing your stories to life when you tell them as part of your presentation requires a] making sure all the elements are there so it supports the point you want to make, and b] delivering them with impact so they are compelling and memorable.

When it comes to building all the elements, we're in luck, because there are clear constituent parts of a story. Simply framed, you need to imagine a mountain:

1. **Exposition**: beginning of the story that introduces character, setting conflict
2. **Rising action**: events leading to the climax, involving attempts to solve a problem
3. **Climax**: turning point and moment of greatest suspense and action
4. **Falling action**: events after the climax that deliver outcomes or impact
5. **Resolution**: challenges solved and view to the future

Importantly, remember, this is a framework. It also doesn't mean the story has to be lengthy.

> *B-Corp had been struggling with inventory before I was appointed CEO; so, my first task was to really narrow down our product assortment. And that was the great unlock; by selling only four things really well, the whole team had more direction, which boosted sales, reduced inventory cost, and established a more profitable business model as part of our company DNA.*

It's a little crude, but all five elements are baked into two sentences.

And it doesn't have to be linear, but it needs all the parts to make sense.

What's important is that you now know there's a science behind the art anyone can apply.

STORY EXERCISE

Let's add an illustration with the elements laid out against a mountain so it makes sense

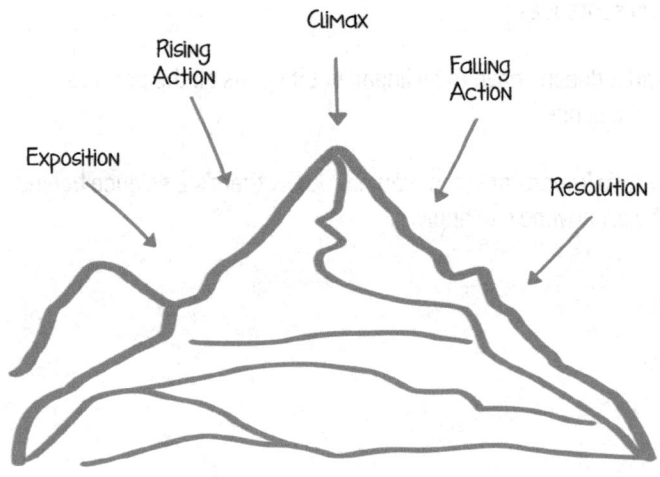

Do the exercise of quickly taking an anecdote and checking you have all the constituent parts

Exposition	
Rising action	
Climax	
Falling action	
Resolution	

NOW PASS
THE POPCORN

Now that you understand the constituent parts of a story, you have to bring them to life.

Take any book, film, or TV show.

The five elements of a story are not broken up equally.

Because depending on the story you want to tell, you might want to spend more time on the exposition (which is what rom-coms do) or you might want to set the scenario quickly to then have lots of drama from the fallout (much like an adventure film).

This will help which parts of the story you take more time over, and which are quicker.

And now you also have an idea of how you will add pace, drama and pauses into the story.

But don't forget, just like a film or a book, you have to tailor it to your audience:

> Very serious business folk: light on drama, strong delivery of falling action, more robust 'aha!' moment.
>
> Larger crowd looking for more inspiration: more light and shade/twists and turns, more empathy, greater ability to relate to their personal experiences.

Again, all of this may seem rudimentary in hindsight but it's an important step.

Adding anecdotes and stories to your presentation is never as simple as *"I know, I'll tell the one about the company turnaround."*

Fail to give it thought and you might miss the key catalysts for change that will be most relevant to the audience.

Fail to add colour in delivery, then it's just a recitation of facts, and it just won't resonate.

Both of these things are important. Even if it's just small nuances in delivery.

Because it services our Golden Rules.

And in doing so will take an anecdote or story from a forgettable subplot to irresistible persuasion.

AVOID A
HUMOUR FAILURE

Humour is an exceptionally powerful presentation tool. Used well, it can bring real colour to your delivery. But the key to the sentence is 'used well.'

When it's not used well, usually when people are trying to force jokes into a presentation, it becomes clumsy and everyone feels awkward.

If you're starting out, or presenting on serious subject matter, use humour very judiciously.

And while it would be impossible for me to 'instruct' you on how to be humorous, I will pass on the three consistent pieces of wisdom stand-up comedians have given me over the years.

Tip 1

Comedians base their material on their personal experiences. In life, comedy and tragedy often go hand in hand. A way of creating a learning moment with humour might best be deployed by focusing the humour and tragedy on yourself, rather than someone else's demise.

Starting with funny personal anecdotes, mishaps, embarrassing moments you're comfortable sharing is a great way to easily bring a humorous angle to your content and also humanizes you through some vulnerability.

Tip 2

'In-jokes' are fine with teams and coworkers but only if everyone is in on it. What can be funny in a social moment can come across as belittling in a more formal environment. You also run the VERY high risk that you joke about something that is upsetting to the individual.

This extends to humour that reinforces stereotypes. In the 21st century, very few comics do this or do it well, and if they do it's usually because they are part of that group themselves. Instead, focus any humour on a topic or experience that is going to be relevant to all your audience.

Tip 3

Profanity is never a substitute for a punchline. While there are significant cultural differences between geographical areas (for example, I might drop a well-timed 'f-bomb' in the UK in the right scenario; I'd never do it in the US). More importantly, to quote *Downton Abbey's* Dowager Countess, *"Vulgarity is no substitute for wit."*

Instead, think about whether a pun or a meme or a pop-culture reference can add levity to your point so that you're making light of it, not just forcing people to laugh.

VERBIAGE DELUGE

Now let's turn to the words you're going to use.

I love language. I like using a panoply of variegated nomenclature wherever feasible.

But again, with all good public speaking, it's never about style over substance.

Yes, specific words/phrases often matter in certain situations.

But an idea that is meant to be simple to digest and easy to execute is rarely helped by feeding it through a thesaurus.

Take a pitch to investors I'm making, and I want to make it clear why people would come to my shop rather than others.

Now you could say:

> *"We stock a broad array of bespoke household products and necessities, exclusively sold at our locations, making us uniquely positioned to service customer choice."*

There is nothing wrong here.

But it's also a lot of gymnastics, when you could just say:

> *"We sell everyday essentials customers can't buy anywhere else."*

Yes, it seems like an oversimplification.

But sometimes applying an Occam's-razor-like approach can be the discipline needed to ensure you deliver your message with impact, rather than people wondering what it was you said.

And while I don't have a philosophical issue with double negatives, I can't be persuaded that:

> *"There is no way that this plan isn't going to be successful"*

is more powerful than

> *"This plan will succeed."*

Therefore, continue to use a broad array of language to bring your public speaking to life, but never do it at the sacrifice of transpicuousness.

ACTIVE AND PASSIVE INFLUENCE

Conventional wisdom would dictate to always use the active voice rather than passive when public speaking.

"That's why I founded the organization in 2016"

instead of

"That's why the organization was founded by me in 2016."

I think this is half right.

The active voice is much more effective when your presentation is either on the shorter side – like a quick progress update as part of a larger meeting – or when the presentation itself is designed to instil a lot of information quickly and land your message with impact.

Examples include annual general meetings, quarterly earnings calls, investor events, broadcast media interviews, especially when your objective is to instil confidence in your strategy.

"A three-stage savings plan will be implemented by ..."

or

"Ten percent above market growth will be achieved by an innovation road map."

is much more influential in the active voice

> *"Today we're implementing a three-stage savings plan"*

or

> *"Our innovation road map will drive 10% above market growth"*

As you're preparing, always go back to the Golden Rules and check that impact hasn't become lost in the edit and add back the active voice where those moments appear in your remarks.

However, with longer presentations, including keynotes, panel discussions, longer print journalist interviews, wedding speeches, etc., light and shade are needed to be engaging.

Balancing the active and passive voice draws your audience in, particularly when telling a story or anecdote and you want to add drama and interest in the person or object experiencing an action.

> *"It became clear that the company was in desperate need of a turnaround."*

> *"I was completely unaware my life was about to be turned upside down."*

Play around with it. As you become more experienced, this will come naturally.

So much so that you'll be able to achieve balance, and balance can be achieved.

SIGNPOSTING

A short but effective technique in your presentation and delivery is called signposting; where you essentially just give your audience a lay of the land, and a real-time progress update.

This is helpful not only to help your audience digest information in sections, but it also stops you from wandering.

> *"This morning I'm going to cover the key learnings from the James Webb telescope, with a quick overview of how the technology is different, what new discoveries we've made, before then turning to the ultimate question: are we alone in the universe?"*

Then as you speak, use them as anchors:

> *"Now before we get to your questions, let me finish with a little about the biggest question of all: is anyone out there?"*

It's simple but effective for prepared remarks, and is also *really* useful for complex answers where you need to cover multiple points and not lose your train of thought:

> *"Investment in AI is critical for two reasons, the advantages it brings to our workforce and its benefit to customers. Focusing first on the workforce ... and then to the second point, customer need ..."*

It doesn't have to be long, and it shouldn't be overly repetitive.

But remember: your audience doesn't necessarily know where you're going.

Signposting helps you guide them, while also making sure you don't lose focus yourself in the process.

I'LL SAY IT AGAIN:
REPETITION HAS IMPACT

There will be those who tell you not to repeat yourself in an interview of any kind.

Yes, for sure, don't repeat the same anecdote multiple times in the absence of anything else interesting to say.

But repetition is a highly effective tool at reinforcing an important concept.

Let me say that again.

Repetition is a highly effective tool at reinforcing an important concept.

I had a spokesperson who naturally said, *"I always want to focus on solid execution and helping the teams 'win the day.'"*

But far from just a throwaway remark, he'd use it strategically to anchor key concepts both in presentations to the board and meetings with his own team.

You knew that was a priority of his. But if he was going through examples, actions or proposals, he'd underscore or tie something together by saying something like *"this is a great example of a change that will ensure the teams 'win the day.'"* People could immediately grasp it.

You don't want to overuse it; otherwise, it can become an empty statement.

But used judiciously and deliberately throughout your talk track, it will reinforce a concept *and* give you multiple proof points to establish why it has impact.

> *"Remember at the beginning we talked about 'clear path to value'? This is another great example of how we make that happen."*

And interviews and presentations are all about delivering your key messages with impact and persuasion; showing them the path to an irresistible outcome that makes good sense.

That's why repetition is a highly effective tool at reinforcing an important concept.

EXCESSIVE PLATITUDES?
NO, THANK YOU KINDLY

Politeness is always important, but it can go too far and take the wind out of your sails.

I remember when I was training at bar school for a sentencing plea in mitigation. I thought I was being so gracious saying *"I'm grateful to my learned friend for setting out the facts, and thank you to the probation team for the very detailed and thoughtful report, which I hope Your Honour has had adequate time to review ..."*

And that's when the judge put his hand up and said, *"Cut the crap and mitigate."*

Punchy, but he was right. None of that mattered.

It was just almost a minute of waffle, when I needed to get to the heart of the issue.

People do it all the time when they're coming in to rep their business or services to a company.

> *"Thank you so much for the time today, and I know you must be so busy, but we really appreciate you taking the time out of your schedule, especially when it's near quarter end ..."*

It's well intentioned.

But we've been talking about primacy and recency … this will become your new primacy.

Far better to get their attention and run with it.

> *"Thank you so much for your time, we're really excited to share this new product with you."*

> *"Good morning and great to see everyone. Now who's ready to talk about tax season?"*

One last time, say it with me: cut the crap and mitigate.

CALL AND RESPONSE

With big, main-stage moments – annual convenings or summits where you have hundreds if not thousands of employees or teammates – rallying cries (like a call and response) can be a great way to energize your audience.

I would like to give two strong pieces of advice.

First, avoid the temptation to get people standing every time you want to launch it, it takes longer than you think and kills the momentum; people should literally be on the edge of their seats.

I once witnessed someone try to make 2,000 people do the hokey cokey three times – painful.

Second, make the response part for the audience as short as you can, ideally one or two words.

For example, you might want to emphasize teamwork.

Call: *How do we win?*
Response: *When we work as a team!*

Makes sense, but it's actually really hard to get people to do it effectively.

Whereas *you* have the control and the single voice.

So, flip and make the response short:

Call: *And what happens when we work as a team?*
Response: *We win!*

Whatever it is, think it through so that the interaction you're trying to elicit is short and impactful and means you'll avoid having to shake it all about.

POLY FILLERS

I'm not going to get into a heated debate about filler and hedging words.

Words such as: *um, ah, like, so, kind of, sort of, right, well.*

Used sparingly, there is nothing wrong with them. They form part of natural speech.

Sometimes they can be a useful moment to add diplomacy to a comment: *"Well, just a suggestion ..."* Or to give yourself a moment: *"So, in my experience, that's best answered by ..."*

The only watch-out I have is excessive and repeated usage. Numerous studies show audiences can perceive excessive usage of *ums* and *ahs* in particular as a lack of preparation.

For example, if you were presenting a bold idea to your board, the excessive use of *ums* would weaken and potentially undermine the perceived conviction of your suggestion.

Therefore, my advice is simple. Keep them in check and avoid overusage.

Two simple exercises can also help this immensely:

1. Ask someone you trust, usually your comms person or a coworker, to listen to a five-minute section.

2. If they hear them, have them take a tally, because it will highlight how noticeable they are.

Alternatively, record yourself for a few minutes and play it back. It's a hideous process listening to your own voice, but it's a sure-fire way of kicking the habit into touch.

Either way, the solution is easy.

First of all, give yourself some grace.

Second, add a pause and then speak with intent.

Either way, you'll improve either because you begin to mix them up and add variety to your speech, or you'll become much more adept at getting right to the point.

QUESTION TIME

On a similar note, fillers often come before responding to
a question.

The media relation section deals in significant depth with the
process of answering and managing challenging questions.
If you're in a scenario where it is likely – annual meeting, earnings
conference, town hall – go there for greater guidance.

In more general terms, if you're presenting in a scenario where a
few questions may come – such as a lecture, keynote, conference
speaking event – simply treat them as an additional part of your
planned presentation.

I don't mean that in a trite way.

Concise answers are *always* the best answers. And so, if you're
thoughtful about your response, you can use them in a natural
way to actually *enhance* your existing talk track.

Refer back to a point you've already made or build on an
existing point.

> *"Absolutely, it's like I was saying in the first section ..."*

And if it's a question on something that's coming up, politely say
so with a smile and grace.

> "That's a fantastic point, and we're going to tackle it in a few moments!"

> "Love it! Remind me at the end because I definitely want to come back to that."

The most important thing to avoid is rushing or panicking to give a full answer immediately.

> **The key to good responses is knowing when to STOP talking, which means being deliberate in what you DO say.**

Speakers are most often thrown because they are in a hurry to immediately answer the question, before the response is formed in the brain.

And this goes equally for easy and friendly questions as it does for tricky ones.

With questions, **always** take a beat, take a pause, take a breath.

And if the answer is complex, use signposting (mentioned earlier) so you can clearly control your response.

Importantly, give yourself time. If you do, your responses will become much more compelling, and even better, additive to the overall narrative.

ACCENTUATE THE POSITIVE

I try to live my life with as few regrets as possible.

One of them is that, over the passage of time and living and working across parts of England and the US, I've lost the British West Country accent I was born and raised with.

I also thought that to be a good courtroom attorney I needed to speak more neutrally to be persuasive.

That's not the case.

I would like to implore you, whatever you do, retain and embrace whatever regional or local accent or dialect you have.

Of course, be aware of it.

Some accents mean you might naturally speak quickly; make sure you slow to keep a good pace. Some accents might mean certain words are harder to enunciate; find an alternative.

Some dialects have particular idioms; make sure they're understandable.

Above all, my luvvers, keep yourself authentic.

Accentuate the things that make you individual and compelling and play to those strengths rather than trying to neutralize them.

SPEED TESTING

Now, you didn't pay (good) money for a book that says, *"Don't speak too fast."*

However, one trap I see people fall into is accelerating their pace when time is against them.

We've all been in that situation where a session overruns and someone says, *"We're running a bit over, so can you make sure we still finish on time."* And hey, presto, because someone was then draining the slide (see earlier note) you have five minutes less than planned.

The temptation is to say, *"OK, I'll go through this quickly."*

You may as well just say, *"I'm going to rush this so don't bother listening."*

You'll see people literally start to put things in their bags.

Remember, good presentation is all about maintaining command of the messages YOU want to deliver.

Far better to briefly acknowledge the time, adjust your focus to the most salient points, and give yourself some grace.

*Author's note: remember not to speak too fast.

"OK team, I know we're a little behind, so I'm going to focus on A and B, and if we make the time up, we'll cover C, or I'll share that in a follow-up note/next week."

The benefit of this is threefold:

1. You stay in control of your delivery and everything you've prepped so you don't garble through it and miss something important.

2. You audience will respond positively to your being mindful of their time and pay you more attention (because they know you're focused).

3. You have created yourself a follow-up opportunity to email or share your materials or even come back another time.

RHYTHM IS A DANCER

The reality is, most of us have natural rhythm in our voices when we talk.

We quicken when we're excited, we slow when we want to deliver something detailed.

However, often when people are delivering a presentation, their speech goes very flat; usually because they're extremely nervous, or they're reading.

And trust me, reading verbatim can turn the most exciting scientific discovery into a recitation of a bus timetable.

However, watch any film, TV show, or stage play, and you'll see variation in speech all the time.

"But they're trained actors," I hear you cry!!! Well, *they* had to learn this too.

Of course it takes practice, but even small variations in cadence will take your delivery from sounding like a railway platform announcement to something that draws your audience in.

And just like actors, the way you develop rhythm is not by forcing it into the delivery, but letting the content define the rhythm. Where do you build to emphasis, where do you cue introspection, etc?

I usually get people to do one of two exercises, so here is a choose-your-own-adventure:

1. If you want a really detailed example of how this works, find online the video of Sir Ian McKellen dissecting Macbeth's "Tomorrow and Tomorrow" soliloquy from 1979; it's absolutely hypnotic.

2. If you want a quicker practical example:
   › Find a poem, any poem; it could genuinely be a limerick.
   › Read the first six lines out loud.
   › Go back and underline the two most important words per line.
   › Then read it again.

You'll naturally lean into where the meaning is important, and that emphasis adds rhythm to create interest.

While these exercises may seem a little highfalutin, they're just meant as a quick trigger to get your brain in gear.

What's most important is that you leave the robot for the dancefloor, not the stage.

PAUSING FOR THOUGHT

Deliberate pauses and breaks in speech are, in my view, one of the most powerful tools in the belt.

Forgive the slightly odd comparison, but in addition to communications, I've also been a long-standing chamber choir director.

There is nothing quite like hearing an entire audience catch their breath as a result of a short, sharp silence after a beautiful chord or melody sequence.

Pauses give audiences moments of headspace to pause, digest, reflect and internalize what they've just heard.

Using strategic pauses after certain key concepts or statements is also an exceptionally powerful way of underlining what you've just said.

The Japanese have a word for it, Ma (間), which crudely translates as the significance of the space between two things. In this instance it can mean both the space between the ideas you are conveying and the physical space between you and the audience.

Obviously, if you use them constantly, they lose their efficacy. But as you look at your talk track, see where a few deliberate pauses will help ensure an important idea sinks in.

The dual benefit of an enforced pause is that it also gives *you* time to breathe, think and reset before moving on to the next point rather than all your ideas rolling together.

And take your cue from the audience, sense them absorbing what you said and move on.

It's a little like stopping at a traffic light or stop sign, checking all is clear, and then accelerating on; it gives you that sense of momentum.

THE EYES HAVE IT

Eye contact is a powerful visual cue for building social links between communicators.

Used effectively, good eye contact influences several perceptual processes in communication, most importantly trust.

But before you say, *"Doesn't staring give people the ick?"* I'm not telling you to stare.

The advantage, nay luxury, of presenting or public speaking to a group is that you don't have to focus on one person.

You can move *steadily* around the room and focus on different people, show that you're speaking to everyone in the room (whether it's three or three hundred) and not only will you build trust, but you'll also build engagement.

And what you'll find over time is that you will start to get visual cues back; you'll see if they're leaning in, you'll see if they're looking bored or confused and then use that to adjust your performance or your content.

If the vibe is right, you can even lean into someone you see nodding along and say, *"You get it, right?"* or find a dissenter and say, *"Not convinced, but give me a moment and you will be."*

In reality, it's no different from any other social contract we build in conversations, it's just done on a bigger scale.

> I had one professor who, when things got technical and he could see us all glazing over, would say, *"Clear as mud test,"* which was a cue for all of us to close our eyes and put our hand up if we didn't understand what he was covering (without any judgement of each other). If he had more than five people in the class with hands up, he'd stop, and we'd go over it.

Audience. Defined. Action.

Find your style, find your approach, but I promise you if you're not building eye contact with your audience, they will only be getting half the picture.

POSTURE, POISE AND MOVEMENT

The overarching point is simple: always stand or sit up straight.

You would be surprised just how much additional attention you can command by doing so.

Try it now: Look in the mirror and then roll your shoulders back, straightening and elevating your posture so you sit or stand taller. Tell me you don't look and feel more confident?

Now, when you're speaking in a large space, there are choices to be made.

Stylistically, some people prefer to talk behind a podium; do so.

Remain standing tall and don't grip on to it for dear life (you'll look frightened) or slouch over it (you'll look like you don't care about being there).

For those of us that like to work a stage and be mobile, do so.

Just don't pace. It's *so* distracting.

I worked with a presenter once who walked the length of the stage to the rhythm of what they were saying:

- step,   step,   step,   turn
- word,   word,   word,   end sentence

They thought it was super-effective ... until I pointed out you could see the front row counting their steps out loud and bobbing their heads in time with his pace.

If you're using movement, the simplest way to think about it is this:

- Command focus by remaining stationary
- Add momentum through movement

I often refer to Alan Rickman and Robin Wright as examples. Their ability to draw you in by standing completely still is a real skill, and it's because body and mind are connected to pull focus.

Then, once you're going, *then* use movement as a tool to gain emphasis.

For example, if you're building up to a point, stopping right before you hit the punchline and delivering it standing still, feet planted and out to the audience, will have a much greater impact than walking through it and then pausing.

Try it. Keep it small or keep it big.

But importantly, keep it intentional.

HANDS AND ARMS INSIDE THE AISLE

This is a topic that sparks much debate.

I'm not averse to hand and arm movement. It can be a useful tool to add emphasis.

But emphasis, itself, requires purpose.

Constant waving of hands and arms around isn't purposeful.

Think of orchestra conductors; they each have their own style, but always to achieve a goal.

Deliberate.
Purposeful.

But sometimes you don't need your hands at all. Especially in moments of calm or thoughtfulness. At those times, hold your head up high, sit and stand with poise, and forget about your hands completely.

And that doesn't mean putting them in your pockets. Tut tut.

Or in front of your mouth. The horror.

Just have them by your side, resting on the lectern, or on the table in front of you.

Just use them, if helpful, to land an important point.

If you want to see the efficacy of doing *almost* nothing at all, watch the video of Leonard Bernstein conducting Haydn's Symphony No.88.

The famously bold and demonstrative conductor manages to conduct an entire movement with just his eyes. No joke. And it loses nothing of the drama of emphasis.

Deliberate.
Purposeful.

Maybe just leave the baton at home.

FIDDLE-DE-DON'T

Simply put; don't fiddle. It's way more distracting than you think.

OK, so my editor said I can't just say, *"Don't fiddle."*

Fair.

So let me elaborate; fiddling means you're not holding your poise.

Because if it's not a *product* of nerves, it *looks like* a product of nerves.

Which means it's critical not to play around with things in your pockets. Don't fiddle with your pen. Don't keep rustling your papers. Don't doodle or play with your phone. Don't rock back and forth on your heels.

And if you have long hair, don't twist around and play with your hair, but instead make sure it's up and out of your face.

Because all these things are distracting and weaken the impact of your message.

Because a nervous-looking speaker is not a persuasive speaker.

You bought this book because you wanted to be utterly brilliant; this is how you'll achieve it.

Calm yourself, harness your nerves, hold your poise.

Focus on your audience.
Focus on your message.
Focus on your delivery.

And all the distractions will go away.

In short: don't fiddle.*

REHEARSE FROM PILLAR TO POST

Always rehearse and run through your presentation/speech at least once, even if you only have a few minutes. *How* you do it is totally up to you.

There is no perfect way to rehearse, because we all process and retain information differently.

You might want to 'read' your talk track in your head, not out loud.

You might want to say the whole thing out loud several times.

You might want to video yourself, watch it back and adjust.

These are ALL valid methods.

But whatever method, always apply the 'pillar and post' technique so you fully internalize the flow of your talk track and the stages and transitions of your key points.

Simply put, make sure you're absolutely certain how you're going to deliver your most important points (pillars) and how you segue between them (posts).

This means, as you're rehearsing, you do two things:
- First, you ensure you're giving maximum impact to the ideas or concepts that matter most.
    > It could be a specific slide, it could be a specific data point, an idea or a recommendation.
    > Know where it is and rehearse precisely how you'll land it.

- Second, by rehearsing the interstitial moments and segues, you avoid breaking your flow.
    > It could be a slide change, a lead-in anecdote, cue for a video, anything that bridges.
    > Know where it is and rehearse precisely how you'll deliver it.

This technique is the key to strong retention and seamless delivery.

People often ask me how I'm able to give an 'impromptu' 30-minute presentation with no notes or slides whatsoever. It's by using this method and visualizing it so that even though I don't memorize each talking point, I visualise the framework and work through it.

This is your secret weapon to making your whole talk track flow, to maintain control from start to finish, and ensuring you lead into each point to deliver it clearly, succinctly and purposely.

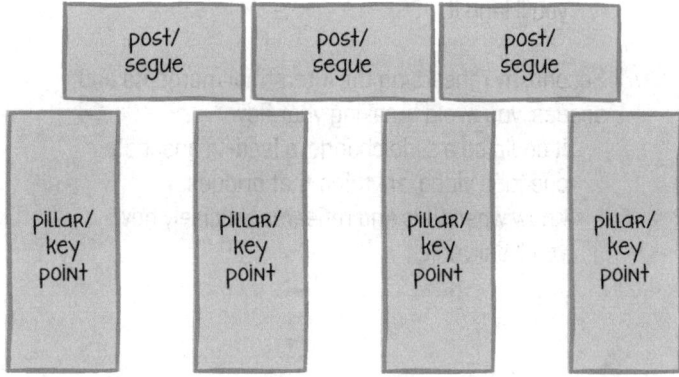

A NOTE ON NOTES

If your speaking notes are in full sentences, you're doing it wrong
- plain and simple.

1. They're too much of a crutch and you become focused
   on *them*, not your delivery.
2. If you have your head down reading, you lose the
   audience's attention.

Notes are, of course, important. Very few people can fully deliver a
30- to 60-minute presentation without any cues.

This means you need a change in mindset: think about your notes
as a map, not a talk track.

As a result, moving away from verbatim prose to memory joggers
does two things:

It forces you to internalize your content more, making you a more
confident speaker
It frees you from the page, so your delivery is more seamless and
your content more impactful.

Again, there is a simple formula to help.

Ask yourself, what do you *really* need to note down to jog your memory? Probably three things:

- **Markers**
  The key themes/points so you maintain your narrative flow
- **Cues**
  Reminders for important moments like anecdotes or slides
- **Highlights**
  Specifics of any details, like key facts or data points

An exercise that I advocate is the following:
1. Write [yes, by hand] your notes on one side of a sheet of paper, avoiding *any* full sentences.
2. Now, take a new piece, fold it in half, and *distil* those notes so they fit *legibly* on that.
3. Now take a final piece, fold in half, then again, and repeat by *distilling* to only *markers, cues and highlights.*

This exercise is helpful three ways:
- it orders your thoughts and embeds your talk track in your brain,
- it forces you to turn prose into succinct notes that act as memory joggers, and
- it leaves you with a useable tool for your presentation – it's small enough to fit on a lectern, desk or even in your hand as a crib sheet.

It's fully possible – because I've taught people to do it – to deliver a full 45-minute speech without slides using this method. Because the process will ingrain it in your memory, and then the notes become a guide, not a crutch.

NEVER PHONE IT IN

A small point, but DON'T use your phone for your speaking notes.

Ever.

Even if it's a non-business event (including wedding toasts, which I now *often* see read from phones – it's someone's big day, for goodness' sake!).

Just don't.

Why?

It's littered with distractions and apps.
It's far too small to glance at effortlessly while presenting.
You'll be looking down too much.
They also switch themselves off, so you have to keep putting in passwords etc.

All in all: messy.

It also, sorry to be super blunt, makes it look like you just cobbled it together five minutes before you took the stage.

Do you think your company board would be impressed with you scrolling on your phone during a presentation? Highly unlikely.

Instead, a small card, note, paper or something similar looks much better, makes you look much more prepared and shows you gave what you have to say some thought AND it keeps your head in the game – the most important part of all.

Tablets, I feel less strongly about in a professional environment. I'm not a complete luddite.

But the bigger challenge here is what to do with them when you're not using them.
If you have a lectern to put it on and refer back to, and you can keep the screen from turning off, then that can be a fairly neat solution.

I will still argue, until death do us part, that a small handwritten card makes you look much more prepared.

And I'm far more likely to say, *"I do! ... agree with you."*

THE AUTOCUE TRAP

Similar but adjacent to my note on notes.

For big presentations – especially if you're speaking at a summit or large gathering for a big company – you may have an autocue-type system.

This is not an invitation or excuse to go back to verbatim notes.

Unless you're reading the news on live TV, which is often updated in real time, an autocue doesn't mean you need to go back to full sentences.

It's a trap.

Because if you are speaking at a big event, the autocue is a tool, not the focus of your attention. That is still, and always will be, your audience. You can't read full sentences and focus on them.

Now. I'm a realist here.

If you have an autocue for a corporate event, you're probably an important person. So, the chances are you (or your comms person if you're in the C-suite) will still write down a full speech for you.

But then you also need to quickly transition to a notes version.

This also prevents two other things that can become incredibly unhelpful:

- It avoids getting out of sync with the operator (because let's face it, there is NEVER enough time to rehearse in these moments),
- And it makes it *so* much easier to make edits or tweaks in rehearsal if you're just changing a word or two, not full sentences.

And to the approach for autocue notes, the formula of *markers, cues and highlights* still works fine and the only additions I'd make are *stage directions*, which are SUPER helpful. Things like:

- Change slide
- Cue video
- Welcome up Oliana (stage right)
- Call and response

> *Pro tip: If you can, colour code differently to the speaking notes so they're easy to scan.*

These are helpful because actions are often the easiest thing to forget in the moment, and nobody wants to be the person saying, *"I'm not sure what's coming up next."*

WALK THE LINEUP

In addition to being good manners, paying close attention to those speaking before you can give you important intel on how to approach your remarks.

Remember, none of us experiences things in a vacuum; your audience is no different.

Take the time to sit in or listen backstage to whoever is speaking *before* you.

And take note on what are they talking about, what's resonating with the audience, is the audience flagging because it's running long, is a common theme coming up you can build on, do you need to adjust anything because someone before you is covering that topic in depth?

These are simple but effective adjustments that can apply equally whether you're a main-stage panellist, a speaker at a wedding, or you have five minutes on screen as part of an all-hands.

It's a *very* good habit to get into.
It also helps manage the nerves and gets your head in
the game.

And if possible, see if you can find out in advance when you're
preparing where you appear in the lineup and after whom.

MIXED MEDIA, MIXED MESSAGES

If you are presenting *anything* that includes video – especially if it has sound – ensure you test it beforehand in the setting you're going to be presenting.

The important word in that last sentence, by the way, was 'you.'

So often incompatibility of microphones or AV equipment scuppers video or multimedia content because the sound doesn't come on, or it buffers, or it doesn't work on the right screen over Zoom or what have you.

And there is nothing more awkward than it happening in a live presentation or pitch. The impact is you will look unprepared even though it is somewhat out of your control.

"Totes cringe," as the kids say. Apparently.

Even worse, though, is when you're on stage and you don't know whether to click to play or whether it plays automatically.

That is on *you*.

So, for any presentation or pitch, make sure you test the compatibility of all the media.

And here's a PRO tip: if you are going to a client's or prospect's office to pitch, always ask if you can arrive ten minutes beforehand to set up and test.

If not, or if you get there and it doesn't work, have a backup plan. A different slide or a static image, something. If it's something like a pitch, you can always send the video on afterward as a follow-up.

Please don't just say, *"We had a video but we couldn't get it to play"* and click on.

As the motto goes: "Fail to prepare, prepare to fail."

PRIMACY AND RECENCY DELIVERY

Naturally I had to close this chapter with some impact, so what better way than to emphasize how a bold delivery at the beginning and ending can be the icing on the cake.

While a good presentation is never style over substance, if you have a strong opener and closer, they *do* need to be delivered with real conviction, energy and even some flair.

Because as well as being memorable, they also bring momentum.

Persuasion starts from the moment you speak, and you want to signal to the audience at the start we're at the beginning of something great and then end by really drawing them in.

Therefore, as you're thinking about your opening and closing points, be deliberate and pay special attention to your pace, style and whether you make the first or last sentence you say particularly bold or striking.

Authors spend a lot of time on it to great effect:

> *"This is my favourite book in all the world, though I have never read it."*
>
> – William Goldman, The Princess Bride

> "It was a bright cold day in April, and the clocks were
> striking thirteen."
>
> – George Orwell, 1984

Both are very different, but the delivery immediately makes you stop and think, "Wait. What?"

Done right, a strong opening and closing, delivered with purpose, will be remembered for years. With that, let me close out with one of my favourite opening lines from life at the bar.

I remember one barrister who was a brilliant storyteller because he would start every tale with the most salacious element. The best example was when he was asked why his nickname at the bar was 'Viscount Alibi' during a judge's retirement dinner.

He began with the immortal line:

> "Well, the hilarity all began when Bruce made the error of
> going on holiday with a woman that wasn't his wife."

To this day I can remember the room going totally silent but for the clinking of everyone's cutlery slowly going down as they all leant in, and the rapt attention the story commanded.

That is how you get people's attention.

So maybe not good advice for life, but good advice for engaging your audience.

DELIVERING WITH IMPACT
- CLOSING THOUGHTS

I hope that this chapter has shown you that there are *multiple* different techniques that can be applied to elevate your message delivery and public speaking ability.

I also hope that it has shown you that there is no single 'style' to speaking well in a public setting.

If building the content is the science, delivering the content is the art.

All the advice in this chapter represents tools at your disposal that you can use.

> As I keep saying: good public speaking is never about style over substance. Stylistic improvements in delivery are all about enhancing a strong narrative, never a substitute.

But they can and will enhance the impact of what you say.

Most important of all, they're not to be forced. They're not to be applied without adapting them to what works best for your personal style.

Because the most important thing of all is authenticity.

This guidance is designed to unlock your potential and enhance your own unique style and personality.
Because authenticity is the most persuasive thing of all.

So, keep coming back to this chapter, especially after a presentation or speaking engagement and ask yourself, *"What worked well?"*

And in turn, stay true to yourself. Lead with personality, truth and authenticity and amplify it with every tool in your chosen toolkit to really bring it home.

Because that's the real secret to delivering with impact.

PANELS
AND
PITCHES

Everything we've talked about so far applies to presenting in a group setting.

The foundations are not wildly different, but the overall dynamic is.

Getting your message across in an impactful and persuasive way means greater attention to those around you and a heightened level of responsiveness.

In doing so, you need to achieve balance. You shouldn't be *trying* to be the sole focus of attention. Nor should you let yourself fade into obscurity.

This means thinking differently.

Whether you're taking part in a panel with people you've never met before or pitching for a contract with a business partner or group of colleagues, group presenting is always a team sport. No question.

And I'm not just trying to be altruistic for the sake of it.

Just like any team sport, even if *you* play amazingly, the audience is ultimately impacted most by the overall game and the result.

Presenting on a panel or in a team pitch is *not* a zero-sum game. Quite the opposite.

This chapter is focused, therefore, on how you elevate and enhance your delivery, while creating an overall positive impact for the collective.

1. **It's not about you**; promote experience and points of view above all else.
2. **Harness the dynamic**; balance the spotlight to enhance the overall impact.
3. **Navigate questions thoughtfully**; manage responses for balanced perspectives.

YOU HAD ME AT 'HELLO'

I love speaking on and listening to panels.

I think they're both an exceptionally dynamic forum for discussing ideas with an audience, and a great platform for getting a message across without all the faff of putting together a keynote.

That said, they still require just as much work.

While this chapter informs how you will prep and deliver in that format, the best thing anyone speaking on a panel can do is to have a conference call with speakers and moderator ahead of time.

Even if you have a PR team that prepares a list of bios of the other panellists (which they should).

And the call can be short. It can be as simple as 20 minutes to do intros, get to know each other, and discuss who's going to cover what.

Or if a call isn't feasible, ask if you can meet 15 or 20 minutes ahead of the panel itself.

The reasoning is simple. By breaking through that initial introduction, you'll automatically be more familiar with your co-panellists.

That familiarity will engender a more natural dynamic, which in turn will enhance everyone's insights and the conversation as a whole.

What's more, if you know someone on the panel is going to lean into specific topics or examples that you might have used, it gives you time to think about alternatives that will make what you have to say stand out in a complementary way.

This applies even if you know people on the panel are going to be taking a contrary viewpoint to you.

An interesting panel is one that naturally builds on common themes through shared experiences while also leveraging respect and openness to different points of view.

Don't be a stranger.

I promise that this small investment is worth the payoff you get in creating a dynamic where everyone shines.

CONTEXT IS KEY

Panels require the same application of the Golden Rules.

But it's important to remember that the context in which the panel is occurring has a greater influence on how you shape your content. Specifically for panels, this means the broader event within which the panel is occurring.

Why?

Because while your panel may be focused on applications for AI in customer engagement, that could be part of a retail conference, an investor conference or a tech conference. All different.

Therefore, the way you shape your answers, and the way you engage the audience, needs to be framed within that broader context. This is exactly what the first Golden Rule is focused on.

I know this might seem a little obvious, but it gets forgotten surprisingly often.

I once saw a brilliant analyst speak on a panel focused on how technology was impacting consumer trends. The problem was that it was a retail conference and all the examples they had prepped related to use of tech in banking and payments. While clearly brilliant, they genuinely looked like they'd shown up to the wrong event.

It also means understanding where your panel comes in the order of events that day.

First thing in a schedule might suggest content and examples focused on setting up the day. End of the day might be more focused on practical application of everything that's been discussed.

It's important.

This relates to internal events as well.

Company town halls or summits often provide a lot of data to employees, including large announcements. This means you need to know whether that news is going to be shared before or after your panel segment and whether to reference it.

Remember, context is key.
There's a time and a place for every message.

PROMOTE YOUR KNOWLEDGE, NOT YOURSELF

The other big mindset shift you need for panels is that it's not about you.

More specifically, while each panel is somewhat different, in general the format of panels is specifically designed for you to share what you know, rather than what you are.

Why?

Because panels are usually focused on a particular theme or topic, which means the fact of your *bona fides* is already established. You wouldn't be there if you were not a thought leader on the topic.

Therefore, in a panel setting, the audience is there because they want to hear about your experiences, your point of view and your advice.

Not just a recitation of your CV and your awards, which can just come across either as bragging or a little bit dull.

Even if it's a format where you're going to be asked specifically about your career journey as part of the discussion, you still don't want to simply recite your career resume.

Instead, always think about how you can lean into the highlights, low points, twists and turns, specific projects or work of note, etc.

Doing so will not only help you stand out as an industry thought leader but immediately make what you have to say more relatable and applicable to every audience member.

ANECDOTAL ADVICE

Earlier in the book we talked about the different ways of bringing colour to your presentations, and all of them are useful in a panel setting.

Facts and empirical data are great in panel, as they help an audience understand the bigger picture, and they are helpful when multiple people are talking around the same point.

They're also a great way of helping draw a distinction:

> "It's interesting what Sarah was saying about customer choice; we see it the other way. Last year we saw the trend reverse with 70% of customers saying they now prefer in-store shopping. That meant we had to pivot as a business by ..."

However, this isn't always easy to prepare for, and sometimes you might have a fact-of-proof point that someone else uses before you.

This is where anecdotes are your secret weapon, as you can deploy them as and when needed.

What I would *STRONGLY* suggest is mapping out what personal or work-based anecdote you can give to each question, so you have something up your sleeve for each question or topic.

And short and pithy is key; it's illustrative, not chapter and verse.

Why?

First, it's the most humanizing of the content proof points you can use. It's unique to you, you can weave a story element into it and can be exceptionally relatable to your audience.

Second, no one else is going to have that same anecdote as you. So, you're guaranteed to stand out.

That means, even if you're fourth to answer the question, you're *guaranteed to have an* original point of view.

> "*I loved how Arvan, Simon and Francesca described it, and it reminds me of an experience I had recently where I had to ...*"

It's a fantastic tool.

And while other talking points will be useful to create variety, anecdotes will always stand you in good stead for a unique point of view.

ENDING STRONG IN
A PANEL SETTING

Regardless of the agreed-upon questions, typically hosts will end a panel session by asking everyone down the line to give some 'closing thoughts' or similar.

You need to *always* be prepared for this question.

Because if you've absorbed the concept of primacy and recency, then this is your last chance to land an impact with your audience.

Simply saying, *"I think we covered it all"* won't make an impact.

So, when you prepare your notes for the content you're going to deliver, get into a habit of jotting down a summary thought that ties everything together in a pithy way.

> *"We've covered lots of topics today with some amazing viewpoints, and it seems to me this all boils down to ... and if we can get that right, we can all ..."*

Alternatively, is there a unique takeaway that you can leave your audience with based on the topic?

There is *always* something. Summary or highlight. Prepare it in advance.

And if you're stuck, one technique I always have up my sleeve is having a piece of really good career advice that is applicable for your audience, especially in a professional setting.

I talk to students a lot, so even if the topic is something very academic or a bit theoretical, I'll still give advice with something pithy like:

> *"The things we've talked about today are all things I wish I'd known when I started my career, so while I have the mic, if I have one piece of advice to everyone in the room it is ..."*

It's not only a nice bridge to all the topics but will give your audience a call to action that is relatable, useable and hopefully inspiring to them.

BITE-SIZE BRIGHTNESS

Now you've outlined what you're going to talk about with context, proof points, anecdotes and your closing all in mind; we need to think about delivery.

The main difference with panels is that you don't have the uninhibited runway of a keynote, where the time and order of delivery is your own.

Instead, the panel host will/should ensure all the speakers have a balance of time.

But that itself will be broken up.

This means that as you think about your content, you need to think about it in bite-size chunks.

Let's do the maths:
30-minute panel, with three panellists, and four agreed-on questions.
Assume two to three minutes for introductions.

That leaves you two minutes per person, per question.
Barely enough time to brush your teeth.

This means you've got to consider two things:
1. What is your overarching narrative that you want to layer through the 30 minutes?
2. How do you break that up into separate points that fit the planned questions?

You see, it requires a little rigour.
Focus only on each question individually and you miss the overarching narrative you want to land.
Focus only on the broad concept and you'll struggle to balance talking points between questions.

Happily, the solution takes just five minutes with a simple exercise:
- Outline the main message you want to deliver and your talking points
- Divide your talking points between the agreed-on questions
- Decide the anecdotes you're going to leverage
- Plan potential closing points

For the record, this applies to webinars and podcasts also, which are a form of panel because the host is also managing their own airtime.

And guess what, if you make your insights bite size, not only will you deliver good sound bites for people to use on social media, etc., you'll have the audience eating out of the palm of your hand!

PLAN ON A PAGE
- PANEL EDITION

For those of us who are visual thinkers, this is the way I capture my panel content as a one-pager.

In this format, you're still grounded with an overarching narrative, you can balance your talking points to hit your overarching message, you have a strong closing point however the conversation goes, and you have anecdotes to deploy as needed.

Use it, try it, play with it.

Overarching Message		Anecdotes
Question One	Talking point • Proof point	• Anecdote one • Anecdote two • Anecdote three • Anecdote four
Question Two	Talking point • Proof point	
Question Three	Talking point • Proof point	
Question Four	Talking point • Proof point	
Closing: **Unique perspective/takeaway**		

RELEVANCE HAS A HALF-LIFE

A tricky but important point.

Sharing the spotlight in a way that endears you to the audience is both a matter of content and timing.

While every panel is different, being alert to the rhythm of the panel, how the host is running it, and importantly how long your co-panellists are speaking for is vital.

There is nothing worse than when you're watching a panel and there is one person who drones on and on, with answers three or more times longer than everyone else every time.

Don't be that person.

Be considerate, be aware and adjust your answers so you're not rambling or hijacking the conversation.

Because people will switch off.

This also includes being mindful of your host.

If they're doing their job well, they should give you visual clues to wrap up or keep going.

On a panel, it's better to be shorter and memorable, rather than lengthy and dull.

VISIBLE LISTENING

Believe it or not, if you're speaking as part of a panel – whether in person or virtually – people will pay attention to you when you're not speaking.

How you behave when others are speaking will influence how your audience perceives you.

Visibly listen.

Yes, you read that right.

Watch the person, turn your body to them, nod, smile if they say something funny.

It's not only courteous, but signals to the audience that you respect the value of others, which in turn commands respect from the audience.

And please – whatever you do – if someone on the panel is saying something you disagree with, don't puff out your cheeks, shake your head, gasp, etc.

Listen, show understanding, and then land a well-placed counterpoint in response.

Remember, you can't control the universe, but you can control how you respond.

REFLECTIVE PANELLING

Importantly, listening to fellow panellists and building off what they say does NOT mean you're not focused on landing YOUR message.

I get the heebie-jeebies when all the panellists are asked their response to the same question, and panellist two or three says, *"I mean, I agree with everything Jim and Sally said, really."*

Yawn.

Especially if it happens repeatedly (because some hosts are not good at mixing up the order of who answers questions ... I see you too).

Always build or pivot to *your* message or *your* unique experience.

> *"I liked Anika's point, and at Fun Corp. we've seen amazing employee retention but applying it by putting in place ..."*

> *"I was laughing when Davu talked about making sure company values are robust, it reminded me of a time when ..."*

> *"I think Devlin is correct, but I also think it can go a bit further when applying wave-particle duality to the manufacturing of toilet paper by ..."*

Or whatever.

Being courteous doesn't mean you can't stand out.

As I keep saying, panels are never a zero-sum game.

A NOTE TO HOSTS

For the sake of the audience and the tedium that can ensue, mix up the order of who on the panel answers each question.

That's all.

A FURTHER NOTE TO HOSTS

If you're hosting a panel, it's not about you.

The more you lean into being inquisitive about your guests, and the less you focus on making yourself the centre of attention, you achieve three things:

1. You'll make your panellists much more at ease.
2. You'll make the panel discussion much more engaging.
3. You'll make yourself look like a host to be invited back.

Of course, be engaging, have tons of personality, but don't fight for the limelight; share the limelight.

Parkinson, Letterman, Norton all have that skill in common; being focused on *their role is* what gets the best out of the guests.

PITCH PERFECT

Over years of being part of – and hearing – competitive pitches across a range of industries and suppliers, there is too much of a cookie-cutter approach.

Individuals and businesses need to stand out and bring dynamism and individuality to stand out from the crowd, and so nothing in these next pages is designed to remove that in any way.

Your pitch should *never* be formulaic, as that usually leads to the least persuasive.

I will, however, state two common failings that get in the way of good pitch content:

1. The lack of *benefit*-led messaging is usually the death of a pitch. If you've skipped to this section in the book, hold the page and skim back to the Golden Rules so you ground your pitch in persuasion, and read page 46 on features, advantages and benefits.

2. There are *always* too many slides. Too much cramming, too much rushing and not enough focus on messaging. Be *really* tough with yourself. Especially in a pitch because you *must* make time for questions and detours in the conversation so you can build a rapport, and you can *always* follow up with a fuller deck after the pitch itself.

The stakes are higher, so your persuasion must be stronger; anything that gets in the way of it needs to be rethought.

And then really bring the passion and *show* don't *tell*. Everything should be immediately, irrefutably and compellingly persuasive.

My favourite lost pitch was the simplest. While we were at a communications agency a potential client simply said, *"Pitch us your wildest, most creative idea."* That was it. The biggest, blankest canvas you could imagine.

We didn't go through the Golden Rules; we got in our own way by convincing ourselves we had to have a well-reasoned, executable and affordable idea, and we stuck to our old ways.

The pitch deck was enormous, and *so much work* went into presenting an idea that was so dull and so lacking in creativity, but it was too late.

In the room we lost the pitch on the first slide. The FIRST slide.

There may be no such thing as a 'perfect pitch,' but there can definitely be a 'perfect miss.'

PITCHING EQUITABLY, NOT EQUALLY

When you have multiple team members presenting in a pitch scenario it's *vital* you think carefully about balance of voices.

And it is a balance.

Whether you have a team of two, three, four or more, you would think everyone gets an equal share of airtime in pitching.

But the reality is that if you're pitching as a team, each of you will have different areas of responsibility, hierarchy and years of experience.

Guess what – the client also knows that and gets that.

More importantly, you need to balance speaking roles as you would balance accountability for the work should you win.

The client will *also* want to know, if they give you the brief, which neck/s to strangle (to use the vernacular) when it comes to managing the relationship – that is the person that should be leading the pitch and having the largest role.

Forcing, and I mean forcing, members of your team to present for an equal amount of time on a pitch simply isn't the right approach. And it adds a lot of unnecessary pressure.

Someone might be very new or junior, so they have one slide.
That's OK.

Someone might cover a very specific area, so they have one slide.
That's OK.

> **As a general rule of thumb,
> don't have anyone present in a pitch on
> a topic that they would not be able to
> answer questions about.**

It will come across as performative. And will look bad if they can't
respond to a question, and even worse if someone has to talk
over them to save it.

Think about the balance as equitable, not equal.

That way everyone on the team is at the pitch, everyone can start
to build the relationship with the people they will be working with,
and everyone can present their skills in the best possible light.

REHEARSAL PITCH

Rehearsing pitches can be an awkward and time-consuming experience.

No one *really* likes rehearsing a pitch. It always feels inauthentic.

But it has to be done.
And by everyone.
No exceptions.

Even if you are really experienced, if you're pitching as part of a team you need to rehearse also.

An analogy if I may.

Imagine Sir Ian McKellen was reprising his role of Richard III in the West End. That play has 52 other characters. Not to mention the theatre crew that makes the production happen.

He knows the script probably backwards by this point. But does he skip rehearsal? No.

Why? Because the rehearsal is for everyone else as much as him.

Everyone needs to know how he'll deliver his lines, where he'll be on the stage, which costume he'll need, etc.

A team pitch is *exactly* the same.

And frankly, even if you are skilled, you probably have some room for improvement anyway.

A proper run-through will let your teammates know what you're going to cover on your subjects, how they might bridge their talk track, how to ensure no one talks over anyone else, how to make sure a slide doesn't get moved too fast.

You get the point. And the psychological impact of seeing a team work well together is hugely valuable.

Therefore, it is far better to muck it up in the run-through and get it right in the real pitch.

And moreover, if you are the most tenured or skilled presenter on the team, other newer members will probably learn from you and benefit from seeing you in action.

Trust me, avoid any winters of discontent, and turn the whole team into a tower of strength.

PITCH DOCTORS

If you can, have someone else in the business watch rehearsals or observe a trial run.

But limit it to just one.
I know, pearls are clutched.

Having objective feedback is important, especially when each of you is in the weeds of your own sections.

However. There is a temptation to run the whole pitch via multiple reviewers.

And then you end up with multiple layers of feedback sometimes conflicting with each other.

And this can mean multiple changes and edits to the document and more stress.

So, what seems like a good idea becomes death by a thousand cuts.

Instead, ask someone to be the pitch doctor early on.

1. Have them involved throughout the process, somewhat at an arm's length, but always informed and reviewing materials so you don't go off course part way.

2. Have them be the person to give the candid feedback in the room during rehearsals.

3. Have them practise asking likely questions of the group.

4. And importantly, have them manage any feedback needed from other stakeholders – so that when you do get feedback it comes in a consolidated single form.

It doesn't need to be an overly complicated process.

But when you're already managing so much to pull a pitch together, you want feedback to be a treat, not a trick.

TEAM INTROS, PART 1

Building a connection with a potential buyer/business partner is vital, but an overly forced attempt with long intros can waste a lot of important pitching time.

With a larger team it gets tedious, with listeners poised in rictus grins waiting for it to end.

Like having all your aunties listening to you butcher Frère Jacques on the recorder at Christmas.

For example, you're pitching a team of six to do advertising for a West End theatre company, there is a *huge* temptation to have everyone do their intro and include their favourite show.

But it always wanders.

> *"Hi, I'm Jan and my favourite West End show is* Les Mis.*"*

And the next person does the same and it builds

> *"and my favourite show, well it was a hard choice actually because I also love* Les Mis*, but then I just went to see* The Music Man *at Leicester but before that ..."*

It's well intentioned, but you'll lose attention.
Remember, primacy and recency.

Kick it up a notch and be creative.

How about take your pitch deck headshot and superimpose a costume over it, or put the show logo next to it, or add your favourite line from the show at the end of the bio?

This authenticity builds connection, adds a little humour and also helps you get to the meat and potatoes of what you're there to talk about.

And if someone stops you and says, *"Wait, I know every song from The Mystery of Edwin Drood too"* [can you imagine?], then you can build on that naturally with rapport in the moment.

Natural, not forced.

I once saw it done really well with a law firm pitching to a football club.

They had a slide with their headshots all superimposed with the club's strip, except one who was a die-hard fan of an opposing team.

The slide came up in the presentation, there was a chuckle and then a chorus of pantomime boos, but it broke the ice, and built an authentic connection.

TEAM INTROS, PART 2

Intros are also *not* about repetition.

PR and advertising agencies are *really* bad at this.

They'll have a team slide up with their names and titles etc., and then everyone goes round the room saying, *"Hi ... I'm Sofia, and I'm an account manager with Thiele PR, and, uhm, I've been with Thiele PR for about three years and ..."*

This is not persuasive. You want the clients to *want* you to be their person.

Instead, focus on your role:
- What will you be doing on the account?
- What unique skills do you have?
- How do you fit into the full team?

"Hi, I'm Sofia. I'll be your everyday point of contact and will lead the media relations programme on the West Coast."

Boom.

Confidence and clarity, and I now know how you fit into the puzzle.

Same with your credentials.

> *"Before Thiele PR, I was at Long PR for eight years,*
> *here I was an account supervisor, and before that*
> *I was an intern ... zzz."*

Instead, what experience do you have directly to the business?

> *"I love the sports sector, having worked with both*
> *Liverpool and Chelsea Football clubs (cue boos),*
> *and I was also part of the 2020 Olympics Opening*
> *Ceremony committee."*

In short, if you want impact, focus on your role, not your title.

TEAM INTROS
- A WAY FORWARD

As a bonus point, and a build on the previous two, I would *strongly* recommend that if you're pitching for business with a team, you send team bios (with photos) the day before.

Sending bios ahead of time does a number of things:
1. Establishes some familiarity with your audience before you meet them.

2. Cuts down on the time needed for intros so you have more content.

3. Provides an opportunity for some levity and creativity.

4. Gives the audience something *you* created to refer back to when deliberating.

The best I've ever seen this done was when I was an attorney, and we were pitching for the retainer with a London property developer.

All of us – I think about six lawyers – lived in London so we sent over a placemat-style one-pager using the Monopoly board, with each of us having our bio nearest the part of the board we lived on.

It was creative but also meant no one waffled on about their mews house on the King's Road (no offence).

And we also could inject humour at my expense, but also a talking point.

I was the only criminal lawyer on the team, so of course, they put me next to the jail square.

It got a laugh, but also was a great segue to my part of the presentation raising awareness of some future legislation changes that had criminal sanctions that the client didn't know about.

Anyway, take a chance (card).

REVERSE IDENTITY

Everything I've said about putting your best foot forward in a pitch applies equally to the people you're pitching to.

Assume they're not going to introduce themselves.

Make sure everyone in the room knows everyone they're pitching to. What they look like, their title, their role, their experience.

At the risk of repeating myself, communication is an audience-defined action.

Have someone prepare a briefing sheet; have everyone pitching read and internalize it – and not just the morning of the pitch. Really ingrain it.

You want to be like the assistant in *The Devil Wears Prada* – know everyone in the room.

It will help you subtly direct certain parts of your presentation to certain people.
It will help you contextualize questions as you know what their area of focus is.
And it will help you build an overall rapport with the team and the individuals.

Now, treat yourself to a cube of cheese before you faint.

DEATH BY TOMBSTONES

There is nothing duller, or more annoying, than an intro section of a pitch having a slide with a collection of 20+ company logos and then whack-a-mole calling out random ones.

By all means include it but put it in the appendix.

Remember the pitch is all about persuasion to your specific audience, so tailor it to them.

What are the three, four or five highlight companies that will make the people you're pitching to say *"Wow ... you work with them?"* and generate some FOMO.

And then be prepared to speak to one or two at most.

> *"We have a track record of working with clients in the retail tech space, but I particularly wanted to call out our work with FoodMart, where we achieved a 50% increase in revenue over just an 18-month period, and we actually have a case study on that a little later on."*

By taking an illustrative, not exhaustive approach, you'll not only manage your time better, but you'll avoid the risk of your audience's will to live slowly ebbing away.

COOLING THE QUESTION HOT SEAT

If you are in a pitch (or presentation of any sort with multiple people), there is an effective technique that helps you manage questions from your audience.

Before the pitch you will, of course, agree who will cover what topics broadly in a Q&A.

However, you still need some management of the conversation, and that means the pitch leader should become a 'chairperson of questions.'

But importantly, that doesn't mean they answer everything. That person should acknowledge and then either respond and/or pass to the person best able to respond.

Now. There are two important processes to making this work, and I DO suggest practising this as part of the prep.

And if no one can answer at that moment, then don't just pass it randomly.

Take the question, acknowledge it with a brief response, and follow up after the meeting.

If the chair knows exactly who to pass the questions to:

A] Avoid throwing someone under the bus by saying, *"Ash is going to answer that"* and launching it at someone.

As the chair, you still need to run interference by creating space so the responder has a moment to frame a compelling response.

So, for example: *"I'll actually pass to Ash as that's their area of expertise, but before I do know we've used our platform for this type of use case before, but Steven why don't you go into some more detail."*

If the question is more random and it's less obvious who should answer:

B] Again, absorb the question and give people a moment. Then look for a signal.

Some people just like their team to acknowledge with a slight raise of a hand. Or a nod. Or sometimes I've seen it where the person who thinks they can respond picks up their pen.

Agree on a cue – hold for it – and pass.

CUT THE SYCOPHANCY

A short point, but for the love of all things, please don't say, *"That's a great question"* after every question you're asked, whatever the setting.

It's really annoying.

Especially in a pitch scenario.

And ends up sounding really patronizing or obsequious.

Mix it up:

> *"I was just talking to a colleague about this the other day."*
>
> *"This is the question I get asked most of all."*
>
> *"It's an interesting topic because ..."*

Then you'll make the exchange more dynamic.

Which is what it's all about.

CLARITY OF SPEECH NEEDS CLARITY OF THOUGHT

No, I'm not just randomly butchering Cicero for fun.

You can't answer a question clearly if you haven't understood it clearly.

One thing to PLEASE do, is if a question comes and you're not sure you've understood it, don't fumble it and guess for fear of looking unable to answer it.

In a competitive pitch scenario, the stakes are just too high.

I remember distinctly one pitch where the person leading it *didn't* chair questions like they should but wanted to be the smartest person in the room.

One of the people we were pitching to was asking a question that the speaker did not properly understand. The person even repeated the question twice slightly differently, but the leader didn't clarify or pass to anyone.

Needless to say, we lost the pitch.

Simply ask for clarity in a discursive way.

"Could you give an example?"

"Is there a particular scenario you're thinking of?"

"Your question is in reference to ABC, have I got that right?"

You're still in command of the presentation, and now you can
e sure to land the right answer.

Don't thank me, thank Cicero.

ONE SINGULAR SENSATION

Often when pitching in particular, a question might have a lot of elements to respond to.

However, do NOT fall into the trap of multiple people responding to the same question with *"Can I just add as well ..." "And another thing is ..."* or *"Could I also just mention ..."*

It looks desperate.

Don't argue with me. It does.

You want to show your listeners – prospective clients, buyers, investors, whomever – that you are in control of the issues.

This is why I always advocate the 'one build rule':

> **One person answers the question,
> and one follow-on response to build if necessary.**

Now, I can hear some of you getting all gee'd up about this and thinking, *"What if I have an important point that also needs to be added because someone missed something?"*

Sure, that could happen. Two suggestions:
1. If another question comes up that you can answer and *naturally* bridge as an add-on, do so; it can actually be effective.

   "We see a X% opportunity for growth here in both domestic and European markets, and apropos to your earlier question about ABC, we actually see upside there if ..."

2. Follow up via email later that day with a note on the pitch and further information on key questions – which is good practice anyway – and give a *short* summary of key points raised and include it.

Always remember, even in Q&A you're in command of your message; command it.

PANELS AND PITCHES
- CLOSING THOUGHTS

As I alluded to up front, there is nothing significantly different about presenting in a group rather than on your own that means tearing up the rule book.

It's not a different set of skills. The Golden Rules still apply.

There is simply one other variable: other people.

The key is using that to everyone's advantage, including your own.

> **It's simply a mindset shift, achieved by moving away from thinking about it as a zero-sum game, and instead remembering that a rising tide lifts all boats.**

Approaching the opportunity with a positive mindset, combined with some nuances in technique and delivery, which are all in service to the audience, is the key.

Remind yourself that your expertise is why you've been invited to speak or pitch in the first place.

Have confidence in that.

Presenting in a group – whether on a discussion panel
or a competitive team pitch – has myriad opportunities
for engagement.

Use them.
Leverage them.

And above all, do so to share in the collective glory and impact
of messages well delivered.

Whether that's a rousing chorus of applause, or a new
client signed.

Now, go get 'em!

MEDIA
INTERVIEWS

Media interviews are possibly the most anxiety-inducing form of public speaking.

Because there isn't much that's relaxing about having a camera pointed in your face or a probing reporter scribble down whatever you say.

First and foremost, journalists are also not typists.

They're not there just to write down what you say because you say so. They have a story they're trying to build, they have audiences to connect to, and they have a brand they're trying to manage.

Understanding this push-and-pull dynamic is vital; none of this is one-sided.

Luckily, there is a structure within the structure to how you approach them.

It's like Inception for messaging.

But instead of a spinning top for a totem, there are simple and effective techniques that will keep you grounded and make your interview go like a dream.

1. **Control your message**, deliver with conviction through point, proof and anecdote
2. **Be constantly quotable**, compare and contrast, contrary viewpoint, future prediction
3. **All tricky questions are navigable**, and it's as easy as A-B-C

MINDSET IS EVERYTHING

The biggest myth to debunk about media interviews is that
they are not actually interviews.
You read that correctly.
That is, to be successful, you shouldn't think about them as
an interview.

They are *not* one-sided.
They are *not* a cross-examination.

Remember, the journalist or broadcaster has asked to speak to *you*.
So, you need to remember *you* are the one in control of the dynamic.

Therefore, it's not an interview; it's a *discussion* that *you* are guiding.

Of course, the conversation comes in the form of questions,
to which you will respond in a courteous and convivial way.

This is not about just steamrolling your agenda. No, no.

But it also doesn't mean you're a slave to their questions.
It's about balance.

Getting your mindset right about the real dynamic at play is the
first and greatest unlock to feeling much less anxious about
the experience. And it helps you realize that YOU are in control
of the message YOU want to deliver.

And, of course, our Golden Rules apply. No takesey backsies.

You are still focused on your audience, you are still focused on the outcome you want to influence, and you still need to frame it in a compelling narrative.

Just because the setting now involves a question-and-answer dynamic and time constraints does not change the importance of the Golden Rules. It's about how you apply them.

Think of it this way: a football player will always play a match to their strengths, but they'll also adapt to the field of play and the opposing team.

And while these skills may require greater refinement at practice, embracing them will make you a master of speaking to both print journalists and broadcasters.

I promise that with time, even someone who has never spoken to the press before can land a live broadcast interview with ease.

WHY ME?
WHY NOW?

When you're speaking to the media, chances are your business or organization has done something newsworthy, or you're commenting on something newsworthy.

Newsworthiness, by its very nature, is intrinsically linked with timeliness.

Chances are if you're being interviewed, your PR team has already done a good job at reinforcing the relevance of the topic and your *bona fides* with the outlet, reporter or broadcast network.

But your audience – the reader/viewer – doesn't see those machinations.

Layering 'why and why now' into your thinking not only significantly enhances the interest and relevance, but it also creates a sense of urgency.

Because if there is *one* thing a journalist *hates* above anything else, it is being behind on a story.

Your role, therefore, is to help them be the first to a story or first to an interesting point of view.

Therefore, when you're thinking through the Golden Rules, you need to frame them in the context of:

Why is the company/organization doing this?

And why is the company/organization doing this *now*?

- Company X announces the acquisition of company Y.
  › Why? What does this mean for the market, and why does what's going on in the market mean this deal makes sense right now?

- Company A launches widget A.
  › What makes this innovation different, and why is this needed now?

- Government Chair D has announced initiative C?
  › What is the problem it's solving, and why is now a pivotal time for change?

Without doubt, when it comes to engaging the media, relevance and urgency are the most potent ingredients that make both the news *and* your perspective utterly irresistible.

ARTICLES AS INSIGHTS TO AUDIENCE

No matter how much you know your topic, an interview with any journalist or broadcaster requires preparation to manage your message and navigate the conversation.

This means gaining insights into the journalist *and* the outlet's readers.

Fortunately, you have the insights at your fingertips, because you can read or watch the journalist's work and that of their colleagues.

If you have a PR team, they will probably have prepared a briefing sheet for you.

(PR folks, please see the last chapter on how to make it a good one as your boss is reading this ... like right now.)

But if your PR team hasn't read the amazing last chapter of this book, your briefing document will probably include links to the three most recent articles written by that journalist.

And while it's helpful to know about other topics or companies they write about, this isn't really what you need to prepare for your interview.

Instead, you need to go deeper and look at the angle and tone of both journalist and outlet to understand a) if it's a topic they cover often and b) whether they have a particular point of view.

This is the key to calibrating your insights as well as what to expect of the interviewer's style.

Your PR team should also have access to media monitoring tools that help with this enormously and can garner insights and data on the media landscape on topics more broadly, so you have a 360-degree view.

While there is no exhaustive list, these are the things to look for when thinking about the Golden Rules:
- What's the journalist's personal view on the topic?
- What's the outlet's editorial (or even political) point of view on it?
- Are headlines positive, scathing, challenging?
- What other types of experts do they quote on the topic?
- How much detail do they go into on topics?
- How do they typically use quotes?

Therefore, as a rule of thumb, three relevant articles are more helpful prep than three recent ones.

KNOWLEDGE ASSESSMENT

Remembering our Golden Rule that communication is an audience-defined action, it's also important to be aware of your interviewer's knowledge on your subject area.

This you can glean *ahead of time* but also gauge it in *real time*.

Lots of acronyms and super-technical terms without context can make you a bore.
Spelling things out in infinitesimal detail can make you sound patronizing.

Moreover, you don't want something important you say to become lost because it's buried in technical speak, or the journalist doesn't understand the context.

So, sense check through the conversation:

> *"Is it helpful if I give you a quick overview of my experience?"*

> *"How much do you know about this charity?"*

> *"Have you spoken to any others about the causes of the Great Depression?"*

> *"Is it helpful for me to tell the difference between semidiurnal and diurnal tide cycles?"*

Remember, this is not about relinquishing control. It's about maintaining it.

By using this feedback loop, you tailor your narrative to what's going to be most interesting and therefore most quotable for the journalist.

But remember, it's still your narrative.
You're just ensuring it all sinks in.

RECORD BREAKING

I'll keep this short: Don't even contemplate going 'off record.'

This book is here to enable you to be quoted in or appear on a news outlet. So, there's not much point me waffling on about how to say things that are designed not to be.

However, flippancy aside, there is a more substantive reason.

Journalists are trustworthy, more so than many give them credit for. But the reality is swimming the murky waters of 'off the record,' 'on background' and 'deep background' are all too lengthy to cover in a book like this and can be open to an honest misunderstanding.

Far better, in my view, is to talk only 'on the record' and focus on being quoted well.

Simply, this means only talk about things or give opinions that you and your organization would be happy to see in print.

> **It's the established 'front-page test.'**
>
> **Would I be OK if what I'm about to say appeared on the front page tomorrow?**

If not, don't say it.
And if in doubt, also don't say it.

And even if attempting anything else is done with good intention, you can't put the genie back in the bottle and say, *"Oh that was off the record, wasn't it?"*

Stick to what you know,
Stick to what you're confident in, and
Stick to what's going to make an impression.

The rest of this guide, therefore, is predicated on getting your interview skills honed and your comments quoted.

TRIANGLE, NOT TRIAGE

Now we've set some fundamentals, it's time to focus on technique.

In a presentation, you control the agenda, allowing fluidity to the order in which you deliver your messages. Speaking to the media is a more interactive dynamic and has greater restrictions on time.

> If you're speaking to a reporter, you might only have 15 minutes.
>
> If you're on live TV, you might only have four.

In either scenario, if you take too long to get to the punchline, get cut off, or lose your train of thought, you've missed your window to land your key message.

And when time is not on your side, it's *very* hard to get back.

This necessitates an intentional shift in message delivery.

Luckily, there is a simple formula that can prevent this from happening, sharpening all your responses and immediately enhancing their clarity.

Welcome to the POINT, PROOF, ANECDOTE structure, where you immediately lead with your main point every time, moving swiftly on to what supports it and makes it persuasive.

We'll cover it in more detail, but visualizing media responses in this pyramid for every answer you give will become indispensable in shaping your media responses every time.

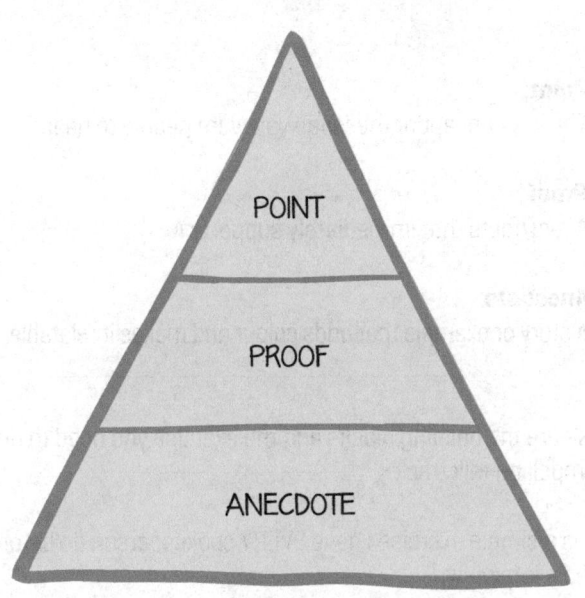

BUILDING
THE PYRAMIDS

To begin with you need to compile the three key elements, which are easy to master.

Point:
The key concept or message you want people to hear.

Proof:
A fact/facts that immediately supports it.

Anecdote:
A story or example that adds colour and makes it relatable.

These are the building blocks and the exercise you need to build a compelling talk track.

This is a simple exercise I have EVERY spokesperson do before a media interview.

On a piece of paper, I draw a nine-box grid: room for three key messages, three supporting facts and three supporting anecdotes. And I have the spokesperson fill them in.

Once you have that, you know you have the elements needed to make a compelling answer – then it's all about delivery.

Let's say you're being interviewed about your flexible timeshare motel business: MoTime.

The **Point** you want to make is:
- The unique MoTime model is completely changing the way people vacation and disrupting the industry for good.

On its own, it just sounds like a baseless claim.

Your **Proof** is then something like:
- Hotel bookings have decreased 60% year over year for the last three years.
- Customers cite 'expense' and 'flexibility' as the reasons for now opting for motels.

Now I know there is a factual basis to your claim.
Now you need to relate it to the audience.

Your **Anecdote** could then be:
- The road trip you took with your kid to college, and the fact you wanted to include detours to national parks at the spur of the moment, but it was tricky/expensive to do so.

POINTED RESPONSES

Now it's just a case of rethinking the order you would naturally deliver each component.

In a social or presentation scenario, you have full control over the time and way you tell a story. You can say, *"It all started when I took a road trip with my kid going to college ..."*

Charming, but with the media the risk of getting cut off before you make your point (how your business is changing the industry) is too high.

> **In a media interview you always start with the point you want to make.**

"MoTime is completely changing the way people vacation and disrupting the industry. Hotel bookings are down 60% sequentially over the last three years, with customers opting for motels because of the lower cost and greater flexibility they offer. I remember doing college trips with my kid, and we wanted to make detours to national parks and make it an adventure, but hotel cancellation fees were so high it didn't make sense; that's why we created MoTime."

The method works because it still allows the story to unfold naturally. It makes your point instantly more compelling because it is supported by clear facts or reasoning.

> **Because even if you get no further than the first sentence, you've still landed your key point.**

Now, it will feel a little odd. It will take time to master. But with practice, you'll excel at delivering a lot of information effectively within a compelling narrative that instils confidence.

If you want to see it done *really* well, watch good CEOs discussing company performance:

> *"This was an exceptionally strong quarter for Blah Corp, with sales up 10%, customers up 7% and profits up 11%, which was fuelled specifically by above-market growth in our widgets division, up over 35% on a two-year basis. Our new partnership with ZenCo is a great example."*

And the best part is that it also works very well to manage not such positive news:

> *"Blah Corp remains an incredibly strong company in the long term. Even with slightly softer growth in Q3 we're still up 5% year over year, and we see tremendous runway in the new products we launched last month, like Blah Candies, which are already exceeding expectations."*

Master this, and you've mastered the most important element of ensuring your responses to the media are compelling and persuasive every time.

GRACE BEFORE BEAUTY

Listen up, CEOs in particular.

When it comes to any commercial enterprise, the well-known adage that 'the business of business is business' remains true.

However, when it comes to all media interviews, it's important to remember that your employees also read and watch the news.

This is especially true with the power of social media amplification.

Over the last decade, the tide has turned therefore, where business leaders have moved away from using media interviews as a beauty parade for *their* efforts and towards a moment of acknowledgement of their teams.

This is also very true in annual meetings and in the US on quarterly earnings calls. Quite often it's the first thing a CEO or CFO says in prepared remarks.

And for any, erm, more old-school CEOs who don't see the value of this ...

Media interviews are a privileged platform to own. There is significant data, including studies from established organizations such as Gallup and the Society of Human Resource Management, that show how much employees value public recognition from their CEOs.

Therefore, a simple piece of advice that I would give, for any company leader, is to remember that interviews of this kind are not a beauty parade for you, but a moment to give grace to everyone who made it happen.

And if you can, do it early on.

> *"Yes, thanks to the dedication and hard work of our teams, this was a stand-out quarter for us and a strong finishing to an excellent year. My sincere appreciation and gratitude go out to the team for all they do every single day."*

That's all it takes.
But above all, make it genuine.

As a wise PR guru always says, 'canned grace' will always sound hollow.
Find your own words, and no copy-and-paste platitudes.

It's a small point, but an important one, and a small change that can elevate both your messaging and your perception as a leader.

RETURN ON INSIGHT

You're investing your time to speak to a journalist, and just like any investment, you want it to have a return. In journalistic terms, that means being quoted and quoted well.

To do that, you have to stand out.

That means now that you've put together the structure and the messages you're going to deliver, you need to give them some real va-va-voom.*

A lot of people will say, *"Just come up with a good sound bite."*
But it's a little more nuanced than that.
Jargon or fripperies won't cut the mustard.
Luckily, just like a P&L, there is a formula.

To be quotable and capture attention, good media commentary requires one of the following:
- Compare and contrast
- Contrary viewpoint
- Future prediction

---

highly technical PR word, you understand.

At an absolute minimum, if you're going to speak to the media, ensure you have at least one of these that you can layer into your point, proof, anecdote structure.

Importantly, these are not a substitute for *quality* of insight.

You still need to bring strong, clear, differentiated opinions or insights to the discussion, but these techniques are how you make those insights quotable.

Having just one of these – or shaping your point of view into one of these so you get a return on your insight investment – will make you instantly Excel in media interviews. *Get it??*

Now we'll break them down.

SOUND BITE 1:
COMPARE AND CONTRAST

This is one of my favourite techniques because it's easy to master and has myriad possibilities.

> The key to the technique is thinking:
>
> *How can I explain this in a way that quickly paints a picture and highlights similarities or differences in a way that's immediately understandable?*

After that, the sky's the limit.

You can use just about anything that sticks with you – song lyrics, politics, economics, your own life experiences – as long as it's pithy, is easy to grasp, and it paints the picture.

This is really the easiest sound bite to master, and you can have a little fun with it.

It also shows your human side if you connect ideas to things you relate to personally.

You can use well-known sayings:
- *Growth for our company is like riding a bicycle: to keep our balance, we gotta keep moving.*
- *Repeating mistakes like this is like tripping over your own feet: avoidable with a little attention.*

You can use similar events:
- *This is not like the election of 2017; there's much more at stake and the playing field is less even.*
- *The US madness for stock gains is being outpaced by the European calmness for fixed income.*

You can use sports:
- *In terms of our company's turnaround, I'm confident we're at the top of the seventh inning.*
- *This merger feels like a 'hail Mary' when they should focus on the 'block and tackle' of sales.*

Or you can go humorous in the right setting:
- *Whipping the votes right now must be like trying to dress an octopus in a string vest.*
- *All they're really doing is picking up pennies in front of a steamroller.*

The only thing I'd avoid are things that belittle other people. *"We're like a one-eyed king in the land of the blind"* – you know the things I mean. They don't pass the 'front-page test.'

SOUND BITE 2:
CONTRARY VIEWPOINT

Just like a lawyer's cross-examination is not about examining crossly, offering a contrary viewpoint is not simply about being contrarian for the sake of it

It's about offering a plausible alternative point of view or outcome, or as a journalist friend always says, *"If everyone else zigs, how would you zag?"*

Happily, most media outlets want a balance of opinions on a topic. Therefore, if done well, this can be one of the easiest ways of getting a sound bite.

> *"It's troubling, but I don't think this is a signal to panic; it's a signal to prepare."*

> *"These global initiatives on climate change are important, but I don't believe anything meaningful will happen until each country delivers on its own targets."*

> *"I know Puddletown Football Club are getting a lot of heat for last night's game, but look how far they've come since relegation and remember, one game doesn't make a season."*

What's nice about a contrary viewpoint is that you can take quite a definitive position without appearing argumentative but instead it is thought-provoking and discursive.

It's all about disagreeing agreeably.

I saw a great one recently in an opinion piece by Colin Stewart in *Gardens Illustrated* on how he wished the modern 'popular' garden design would think more long term and about the garden's natural evolution rather than how to protect a perfect stasis.

Taking a contrary viewpoint is what made his article print-worthy in the first place. But he also used his point of view to close the article in a pithy and memorable way, simply with the sentence:

"Aftercare shouldn't be an afterthought."

Bright. Brilliant. Irresistible.

In short, if you give them something to think about, you give them something to quote.

SOUND BITE 3:
FUTURE PREDICTION

Arguably the simplest. It's exactly what it says it is.
But people get worked up about it.

"But what if what I say doesn't come true?"

If you question whether your perspective might not come true,
and that someone might read it in a year's time, hunt you down,
thumb their nose at you and giggle about you behind your back
with their friends, then you're thinking about it the wrong way.

The key to a future prediction that makes a good media sound
bite is highlighting a potential outcome that is clear, fact-based
and makes people think.

It's not: *"It's clear the whole economy is going to tank."*
It is: *"If this path continues, the risk of recession
            is certainly more elevated."*

It's not: *"You're going to see FoodMart definitely
            out-comp last year's sales."*
It is: *"If the current consumer environment continues,
            we'll definitely see an up-side for the year."*

And think about what the call to action is for your audience; it can become incredibly powerful.
David Attenborough is stunning at this.
When talking about climate change, he simply said, *"If we don't act now, it'll be too late."*

Clever. Compelling. Memorable.

It's a nice technique because it can work very well outside of media interviews to create a sense of urgency with employees and stakeholders also.

> *"I know that to everyone here $XM dollars incremental sales this year may seem completely unachievable. But get this: if we get every customer to spend just 35c more, the price of one soda can, then we not only meet it, we beat it."*

Future state, clear path, relatable to the audience.

THEY DON'T
GOT IT INFAMY

Now, let's turn our attention to tricky questions.

Journalists are nosey. Journalists are provocative. Journalists are in a hurry.

They don't have it in for you. Usually.

The reality is, they simply want access to information others do not.

To get that, they want succinct responses (so they can get to publishing), and they want to have insights that come from an authority on the subject (because that's what gets them and not their competition readers).

They're probably also working on multiple stories on multiple deadlines.

Understanding that *this* dynamic can make them a little pushy or brusque is important.

If you're speaking to them to give your insights on a trending topic, assuming the journalist is going to give you a hard time will dampen the quality of your insights, your energy, your passion – the very things that will make you a good interviewee.

Of course, prepare for difficult questions but assume positive intent.

And if the journalist is brusque, direct, seeming to not listen (because they're probably taking notes) or hurried ... *still* assume positive intent. It's them, not you.

AVOID HOSTILITY AT ALL COSTS

Difficult and challenging questions will come.
It's grist to the mill if you're a senior leader giving media interviews, especially broadcast.

Happily, there is a formula for this also, but before we get to that, two unbreakable rules.

The first rule of handling tricky questions is: NEVER be hostile back.

I'm not here to evangelize philosophical practices, *but* one principle that I hope this book has instilled – but should definitely instil in this area – is one of stoicism.

The basic principle of which is this: we can't control all the world around us, but we can control how we respond to it.

This is vital in a media interview.

When you are asked hostile, difficult, rude, blunt or negative questions, never, never, never lose your cool.

Don't raise your voice. Don't tut. Don't shake your head. Don't say, *"What a stupid thing to say."*

None of it.

Remember, YOU are in charge.

You are controlling the responses, which is the part that will be quoted.

So, keep calm, collected and poised at all times.

NEVER SAY
NEVER AGAIN

The second rule of negative and hostile questions is: NEVER repeat the question back.

This is a technical and important point.

The reason is simple: well-prepped interviews can result in a negative angle simply because the interviewee has imitated that same language.

If the *journalist* says it, it's just a question.
If *you* say it, you're on the record.

Let's take a simple yet loaded question:

Q: *"Mr Bloggs, as the team's coach, do you think it would be fair if Mudtown Football Club gets relegated over the claims of certain players cheating?"*

A: *"I'm not sure it would be fair to relegate the whole team because some may have been cheating."*

A reasonable and reasoned response.

However, the quote is now useable in a headline:

> *"Mudtown FC coach doesn't see cheating as a 'fair' reason to relegate"*

> *"Relegation due to cheating not 'fair' according to Coach"*

You see where I'm going.

This is a technique that journalists and lawyers are good at and it's used for a reason – to goad and to legitimize their version. Which may or may not be right.

But in a media interview you're here to tell YOUR version.

So how do you manage these questions?

THE A-B-CS OF TRICKY MEDIA QUESTIONS

The A-B-C approach is the fundamental building block and structure so you can politely but effectively navigate from any difficult or sh*tty question.

A - B - C

Acknowledge – Bridge – Communicate

This is an approach that 99.999999%* of PR gurus will agree is the best way to navigate tricky media interviews.

I'm going to take each in turn so it's digestible, as this is a complex concept that, to be utilized effectively, needs to be as ingrained as, well, your ABCs.

*not based on actual research but I'll still stand by it

A: ACKNOWLEDGE

Avoiding the question completely looks evasive.

Dare I say it: politicians are guilty of it often and it doesn't inspire trust.

Instead, without repeating what was put to you, *briefly* demonstrate that you're responding to the question, so you can then guide quickly to where you want to be.

This should be about 10% of your response.
Some examples include:

> *"What's critical to remember is ..."*

> *"What I'm focused on right now ..."*

> *"Let me put things into perspective ..."*

> *"What readers/listeners should know ..."*

> *"These are complex issues ..."*

This is not meant to be an exhaustive list, but it's illustrative.

Find the few you're most comfortable with, and practise with a response that doesn't repeat the question.

B: BRIDGE

Simply put, the bridge is a phrase or statement that follows your acknowledgement and naturally navigates to what you want to talk about.

Typically, when you bridge, you're going to do one of two things:

FLAG the different issue that you consider more relevant or ZOOM OUT so you can get out of the weeds of a specific example and talk in more general terms.

FLAGGING could be:

> *"It's an interesting idea, but I'm more focused on what next year looks like ..."*

> *"I wouldn't put it like that, I think the progress we've made to date is ..."*

Alternatively, if the question is concerning something not in your area of expertise you can be more declarative.

> *"That's not really my area of expertise, I'm much more focused on ..."*

> *"I can't speak for the organization, but my personal view is that ..."*

ZOOMING OUT could be:

> *"It's critical to remember there's been an industry-wide challenge over the last two years ..."*

> *"Let me put that into perspective, over half the organizations in our sector ..."*

Zooming out is a very helpful technique; I often equate it to pulling a rip cord from a parachute. It can get you out of free fall.

Just remember, you still want to zoom out to an area you want to talk about, not a bigger negative problem!

You don't want to pull the rip cord only to catapult into outer space.

C: COMMUNICATE

Once you have navigated out, now is the easy bit: take command of your message as if it was the question you wished you'd been asked.

Let's go back to Mudtown FC.

Regardless of the question – good or bad – the point of the interview is to demonstrate you have faith in the team and you're focused on the game.

Q: *"Mr Bloggs, as the team's coach, do you think it would be fair if Mudtown Football Club gets relegated over the claims of certain players cheating?"*

*"**[A]** What's important is that **[B]** as their coach I'm laser-focused on the team's performance on the field **[C]** and I'm confident we'll soon be back to the stellar playing the fans expect from us."*

Or

*"**[A]** These things are complex **[B]** but fans across all of the premier league deserve great games this season **[C]** and no one will be thinking about relegation when they see the hard work we've put into training show up on the field."*

The key here is that you're managing and retaining control
of the messaging.

You're keeping it in context of what you're being asked.
The **bulk** of your response is on the thing *you* want to be
talking about.

And if the journalist starts to get tricky and say, *"Yes, but ..."*
or *"But isn't it the case ..."* to keep going back, stay your course.
"Like I said ...", "Again, the key issue here is ..."

They'll get the point.

PRACTISING THE ABCs

This book, as I've said before, is an illustrative guide.

The examples above, I'm sure, could be tweaked *ad infinitum*.

That's the point. You're thinking.

The important part is the A-B-C system is the foundation of a skill to practise and sharpen.

Think of it as building blocks. If you do, even the trickiest, meanest, most closed-off and leading questions designed to put you on the back foot become easily navigable.

> *"Congressperson/Minister, these latest incidents prove, do they not, that the system is completely broken?"*
>
> *"[A] What your readers need to know is [B] that we need systematic change across all levels of government so as to have the biggest impact, [C] which is why this bill I've announced today is so vital because it will ..."*

> "Ms Floss, doesn't it seem like now's the time for you to step down from ThieleTech? Surely investors must be getting frustrated with the stock price and competitors stealing ground?"

> *"[A] The reality is the whole tech sector has seen cyclical pressures [B] but looking at the ThieleTech's performance in perspective, [C] software sales are up 38% since I started, we've taken significant market share, and we have a clear plan for profitable geographical growth this year – that's what I'm focused on delivering."*

> "Your government is responsible for the worst inflation this country has ever seen, isn't it?"

> *"[A] It's important to remember [B] that inflation was already rising significantly before we took office, [C] which is exactly why we're taking the decisive action to correct that by implementing a new initiative that will deliver ..."*

In short, just like ABCs are invaluable to read and write, so too is this technique.

NO, NO, NO, NO COMMENT

I get asked this a lot.

"Can't I just say no comment and shut it down?"

No, not unless you want to look like you're agreeing with the statement or trying to hide.

It's also a missed opportunity to get your side of the story across.

So, rely on the A-B-C approach.

I *will* concede that in certain cases where there are ongoing legal investigations or matters, your lawyers will advise you not to comment on that.

My advice, being a lawyer also, is that it's far better to say something like:

> *"I can't comment on ongoing legal matters/any legal matters."*

My general experience is that journalists won't push the point, and readers are more understanding of an answer like that.

That said, even with that response, you still bridge. The bulk of the answer still has to be on the message *you* want to deliver.

> *"**[A]** I can't comment on ongoing legal matters, **[B]** I am however focused right now on **[C]** making sure that ..."*

SILENT WITNESS

There is another technique that can be deployed in tricky scenarios: the sound of silence.

We've all cringed at the site of an awkward first date at a restaurant when the couple isn't talking. The temptation to send over two martinis to warm things up is very real.

I've grown both uncomfortable and thirsty at the thought.

Why?

Because as humans we naturally hate awkward silences.

Unfortunately, lawyers and journalists have worked this out and can use it as a tool.

Barstewards.

Sometimes when I was cross-examining, I'd leave a long pause and pretend to look at my notes. That would leave the witness in silence on the stand.

And what happens, they start to talk. And it's not purposeful, it's not planned, because it's not in response to a question. And that's when something is said that wasn't intended.

Journalists can do it too. They leave you hanging in the hope you might say a bit more. And invariably it's not something you planned to say.

So, don't.

Remember, you're in control.

Get uncomfortable with a few moments of silence. Just wait. Stay in command.

And if it drags on, simply ask politely, *"Did you have another question?"* or *"Was there anything else you wanted to cover?"*

Then get back to the plan.

WHEN THINGS GO REALLY WRONG

CEOs in particular: listen up.

Public apologies in the media when there has been a significant crisis are a complicated issue beyond the scope of a short skills-based book like this.

That being said.

steps on soap box

What I will say is that, in the 21st century, reputation is everything.
Mishandling a crisis or issue can significantly impact an organization.

Lawyers and PR pros have come to understand that acknowledging and taking responsibility for a serious crisis or issue is not equal to an admission of guilt.

In a real crisis, every response and every moment counts. And you need to trust your PR team.

Clearly something as serious as, say, a fatal accident of some kind can't be responded to with *"My focus is on company performance ..."*

In essence, three things need to happen:
1. The top person of the organization has to be the spokesperson (usually the CEO).

2. That person must acknowledge the issue and avoid hubris.

3. And at the same time demonstrate how they will overcorrect and take responsibility to avoid a repetition.

Or in shorthand: "*We mucked up, we're devastated, we're sorry, and it won't happen again.*"

Subterfuge of any kind is spotted and jumped on and simply makes it worse.

Instead, an unequivocal and genuine apology and promise to put it right is met with at least a calm acknowledgement of error and the start of forgiveness.

COMPETITIVE EDGE

This chapter has included a lot of technique, so these last few pages are more practical guidance based on bitter experience!

And this one is a big one.

No matter how tempting it may be, do not use an interview as an opportunity to slam or criticize your competition, even if goaded.

First, it's just not a good look. At best it looks defensive, at worst it looks petty.

Second, you run a real risk of saying something that's incorrect or misinformed. Then you are in a whole world of pain.

Third, and most importantly, focusing on your competitors is a missed opportunity to focus on *your* message.

Remember our point, proof, anecdote model? The point is not to give your competitor any airtime; the point is to reinforce WHY you're better/stronger/more profitable, etc.

So, get to that FIRST.

Q: *"Your competitors seem to be gaining more market share purely because they're priced better than you are?"*

A: *"It's a dynamic market and we've pivoted fast, which is why over 70% of our assortment is now at everyday low prices, and we're seeing the impact of that with increased foot traffic ..."*

And if it is very direct, use the A-B-C approach:

A: *"Other charities in this space have said you're simply 'out of touch' and not solving anything."*

B: *"I'm not focused on critiques, I'm focused on getting the aid to where it's needed. Last month we delivered 30% more food donations to these communities than we did in January, all because we have a clear direction and amazing teams that are focused on ..."*

This is the point of why you're doing the interview anyway. And it's far more persuasive because you're doing it in a way that keeps your head held high, using it as just another opportunity to reinforce your message.

TONGUE UNTWISTERS

I talk about various elements of rehearsing throughout this book, which some of you might choose to ignore.

Fine, be that way. *blows raspberry*

However, the one thing I will implore you to always do for a media interview is this. Take your trickiest or most complex message or proof point to land and say it out loud several times over.

Why? Familiarity often leads to complacency.

Time and time again I see strong interviewees stumble because they flub the delivery of a complex or important point because they haven't practised or perfected the delivery beforehand.

And then it's too late. Because the impact is gone.

It could be something simple like the key numbers relating to your company's performance:

> *"We're confident that the 50% reduction in workforce today will yield a 60% increase in productivity and 80% improvement in EBITDA."*

Get the numbers mixed up or fumble the delivery and your stock will go the complete wrong way.

Or it could be something like a complex scientific or technical term.

I used to work with a brilliant trilingual German scientist whose area of expertise didn't translate easily between an English acronym, a lengthy title in French and a long compound word in German. It would trip her every time and then she was thrown off throughout.

The point is, it's simple and it's avoidable.

In the scientist's case, it meant that her prep was simple: repeat her job title three times in the language she was going to present in.

The simple act of recitation grounded her and immediately clicked her brain into gear.

So, now all you have to do is make sure Ökologischverträglicheenergiequellen just rolls off the tongue.

Einfach.

SOUND AND ILLUMINATING ADVICE

As we close the chapter, a few notes on broadcast-specific interviews if you're doing them via video from home or your office.

Assuming you don't need me to tell you not to have a light source like a window directly behind you so you're in shadow or to have any rude artwork on your wall, I simply need you to do me *one* favour.

Buy yourself a plug-in microphone (so you can be heard clearly) and a ring light that can be adjusted for height and warmth (so you can be seen clearly and not in shadow).

This is an easy online purchase that I'm still amazed people don't do.

And then you're panicking five minutes before you go live, stealing lamps off people's desks and trying to find a way to get the levels right. And now you're stressed and sweaty. And there is no makeup team ...

Buy it, test it and have it handy.

Just make sure the microphone connects to your computer and test it for feedback in good time before you dial in.

Because let's face it, why read a book about being utterly brilliant with the media if people can't see or hear you when you do?

DISTRACTION FREE

Additionally, whether you're at home, in the office or in a studio, remove all distractions and politely tell anyone around you in advance that you're going to be on live broadcast.

If you've never seen the video of Professor Robert Kelly being interrupted during a live BBC news segment, then put this book down, go and watch, and then come back.

I'll wait.

chuckles while even thinking about it

Now you know why. Although it's stinkin' cute.

And it happens all the time.
You'd be *amazed* how many friends text or even video-call you when they see you on live TV.

So, put all mobile phones, pagers, egg timers and Tamagotchis away. Better yet, if you're in a studio, just give them to your PR person.

The added benefit is it stops the mobile device spoiling the line of your jacket.

And for goodness' sake, if you're video conferencing in, shut down all email, text, Slack alerts and what have you also.

You NEVER want to run the risk of it pinging right when you're saying something erudite, or a message popping up on the group chat to complain that Alan forgot it was his turn to bring biscuits for the team again.

You can deal with Alan later.

GETTING YOUR GOOD SIDE

People often get very confused about where to look if they're in a TV studio being interviewed.

The answer is simple: towards the person asking you the question.
The cameras and the crew are well rehearsed at capturing the guests.

Remembering this is also helpful to combat nerves, as you can focus on it being a conversation rather than an interview.

And if you're appearing via a link, look at the camera, not yourself on the screen – that means turning off or blocking any self-view so that your eye line isn't drifting off to the side.

Also ...

No swivel chairs.
We want your best side, not all sides!

This means that if you're at home or in your office, change your chair to anything that is static. Keep still. Don't fidget.

And if the TV studio is mean enough to pop you on a swivel chair, resist *every* temptation to wiggle, because every move you make is exaggerated on camera and just makes you look nervous or unsure.

Sit still, plant your feet, and if possible, rest your arms/hands on the desk.

THE REAL TRICK QUESTION IN ALL MEDIA INTERVIEWS

And now, for what I consider the most valuable piece of advice I can ever instil.

When you speak with a journalist – usually print but it happens in broadcast also – they very often end with *"Thanks, was there anything else you wanted to cover?"*

No matter how comprehensive the conversation was, this is a trick question.

Why?

Not because it's mean, but because saying *"No, we covered it all"* is the biggest missed opportunity in a media interview of any kind.

Remember the doctrine of primacy and recency.
You don't want the last thing the journalist hears you say to be nothing.

Instead, always do one of two things

1. Use it as an opportunity to secure a message you didn't *already* get to land.

   "Well of course we didn't talk about the work our foundation has been doing in this area ..."

   "Did you know that we actually just launched a new X that solves Y this year ..."

   "Are you covering the new rule changes that might impact the healthcare sector ..."

2. Or, if you covered everything in the interview and there is nothing new, then take this moment to *reinforce* your strongest point:

   "We covered a lot, but the real key takeaway here is X ..."

   "That was a great conversation and talking about Y in particular feels like the main issue here."

   "I really hope overall you got the impression that A is the future of B as this area develops."

You're in control. So, make sure you get all your points across or reinforce your strongest point.

Any alternative is a waste.

Don't confuse this question for a trick, turn it into a treat.

MEDIA INTERVIEWS - CLOSING THOUGHTS

If I have one wish, it's that this chapter has simply taken the fear out of agreeing to a media interview.

I can't stress enough just how much it's like any other form of public speaking. It's still about delivering your message in the most compelling way that lands with your audience.

> The only thing that's different about a media interview is the mindset shift needed to turn the scenario into a platform that works best for you.

At the end of the day, while being good at speaking to the media requires an additional investment in time and refinement of technique, the payoff is significant.

And not just because a strong message or national or international media has the ability to influence millions.

But because you, your PR team and your colleagues will all get enormous pride from seeing you represent your organization in the best light possible with your quote in a paper or seeing you nail a segment on TV.

Just remember, if ever you're feeling unsure:
- You're the *expert* that is bringing the interview to life.
- You're *fully in control* of your responses.
- You're the one that can turn the scenario to your *advantage*.

Now.

Going live in three, two, one ...

NOTES
FOR
PROS

Just to be very clear, if you are a comms or PR pro, you're not resigned to reading only this chapter.

This whole book is designed for both speakers and the teams that advise them.

In the same way the guidance is useful for those taking the stage – literal or metaphorical – it's useful for the pros supporting, advising and counselling them.

This section is, however, focused on specific advice that will help you provide more effective and reliable support for your speakers.

Candidly, it's based on mistakes that I have made and learnings that I have developed from my own shortcomings.

Without doubt, PR and comms leaders and functions are becoming more valued by CEOs and senior leaders of businesses and organizations.

What I hope above all is that *everyone* reads this chapter so that everyone shares a common language, in turn making practice and feedback more effective.

In doing so, it will help elevate everyone's thinking and approach so that spokespeople become brilliant, and you become indispensable to your leaders and an influencer in your own right.

1. **Be more prepared than your speaker**; reliability is the key to success.
2. **Work all the way to the final goal**; the job isn't complete until the quote is printed or aired.
3. **Feedback is a responsibility**; define a common and consistent approach using proven methods.

UNDERSTANDING YOUR ROLE

As a PR professional (inhouse, agency, whatever), your job is not to secure the speaking/interview opportunity.

Let me repeat that: your job is not securing the opportunity.

You need to focus on the outcome, which means your job is ensuring the coverage of the interview – whether print or broadcast – delivers the message your spokesperson/spokesperson's company needs.

That starts with finding the right newspaper, blog, podcast or industry event for sure.

But if your spokesperson isn't well briefed, well prepped and able to effectively deliver the messaging you need in a way that is clear and compelling, so it becomes the sound bite or takeaway of the piece, then you haven't done your job.

Simple.

And sometimes a good setup but with flawed execution can actually lead to negative coverage and then you're in a worse position.

That's the responsibility.
That should also be your north star.

As you think about your job and your career growth, do *not* focus on media opportunities secured *EVEN* if your boss [whoever that is] says the number of opportunities secured is the KPI to focus on.

Instead, focus on stewarding and supporting your spokesperson throughout the WHOLE process and managing ALL the parts that need to come together so the output is utterly brilliant.

BE MORE PREPARED
THAN YOUR SPEAKER

At school, our head teacher used the same quote from Thomas Edison at the first all-student assembly of every school year.

> *"Success is 1% inspiration, 99% perspiration."*

This is something that has always stuck with me. And I credit my career success, as a barrister and as a communications consultant, to the application of that maxim.

Nothing more, nothing less.

As a PR or communications consultant, this translates to preparing your spokespeople for interviews or presentations.

And specifically, it means knowing your spokesperson's talk track, presentation, speech, proof points and sound bites as well as – if not better – than them.

Your job is not to give them something quippy to say and then push them on stage and say, *"Good luck."*

No, no, no.

It's only by working on the interview or speech as hard as you expect your spokesperson to do that you are really doing your job.

Because that way you're ready to respond, assist, confirm, correct whenever you need to.
Your CEO, CFO or whoever should never turn to you and ask, *"What's the stat again?"* and you do not know, or you have to start scrabbling for the talking points on your phone.

Do the work. Put in the time. Before, during and after the speaking/interview opportunity.

Because your spokesperson did.
And they're the ones under pressure.
And they are the ones that will need your support when it matters most.

Do your homework, and if you prepare as thoroughly as your spokesperson, you'll not only help *their* image, but you'll help *your own* too.

CAMERA SHY, CAMERA TRY

There are many people – and I mean *a lot* – who are confident and eloquent public speakers who could address great pantheons of people only to turn into blancmange the moment a camera is pointing at them.

I think I've seen more people lose their nerve this way than any other failure to prepare.

A small but important thing to remember is if your exec/ speaker is one of those people – or if they have not had camera experience before their live event – practise with them.

And it can be very simple, like using a smartphone or video conferencing tool.

Point the camera at them, give them a hot seat, and play the part of an anchor.

While this may seem daft, getting that shock out of the system a few times before the main event will help WONDERS.

Remember, encouraging good practice is what we're here for.

BRIEF BRIEFING SHEETS

Media briefing sheets: oy oy oy.

I know you hate them. But they're arguably the most important deliverable.

Execs are *super* busy, so your briefing has to be punchy and powerful.
I could write a whole book on the topic, but I'll follow my own advice and keep it short.

1. Remove repetition and redundancies (I see this ALL the time)

Briefing Sheet: Interview with John Smith, deals reporter at *The NYT*

This is a briefing sheet prepared ahead of your interview with John Smith, deals reporter at *The NYT*

About John Smith, deals reporter at *The NYT*
John Smith has been a deals reporter at *The NYT* ...

Please end the misery.

---

2. Provide the most *relevant*, not the most *recent* articles/coverage, and add a sentence as to WHY

> *John has covered crypto three times this year (articles below) and tends to write with a bias on the overvaluation of recent M&A deals in the space.*
>
> Your media monitoring and analytics tool is crucial here but so is using it thoughtfully.

3. Frame the proposed talking points like talking points, not just big narrative copy and paste

> **Talking Point 1:**
> *Our business performance compared to competitors this year shows why we're the number one restaurant destination for consumers*
> - *Sales were up X% year over year, with B brand being one of the most popular*
> - *We saw improvement in the bottom line, which is why we could invest in C*
> - *Our ABD advert was one of the most watched in Superbowl history*
>
> *Anecdote: Associates in our NYC location report that customers are loving the new XYZ product, especially around the holidays*

FEEDBACK IS A GIFT

Practicing presentation and media skills is daunting.

As the trainer, your job is to help elevate your spokesperson's skills and instil confidence. Simply replaying a list of all the things that need fixing is often unhelpful and disparaging: *"and this, and this and this, oh and then you did this."*

Therefore, the next pages cover two different training methods that generate *instant* improvement.

The **build method** is for newbies to public speaking to improve while maintaining morale.

The **focus method** is for those more seasoned and focusing on areas of improvement.

Importantly, this is about providing feedback on technique.

Applying these two methods does not negate the need for you to know the facts and stats as well as your spokesperson does, and to politely correct if there is an error made, like the wrong sales number being used, or growth percentage, etc.

Your enduring obligation is to always make sure things like that are correct.

THE BUILD METHOD

I once had the privilege of seeing a very well-seasoned professional theatre director rehearse an amateur group of actors.

They did their scene, and there was lots wrong with it. However, this director did something incredible. She gave no negative feedback or criticism but went to each performer and focused on the one thing of their performance she really liked. It was simple things like *"I love how you were physically animated on that line; do that throughout"* or *"You had great facial expressions when Sam was talking; try reacting to all the characters just as much."*

She then asked the troop to do the scene again with that feedback and, you guessed it: instant transformation.

Both in terms of quality of performance and confidence.

Therefore, if you are giving feedback to someone who is very new to all this presenting malarky, use that method.

The person is probably already super nervous, worried about what people will think and overthinking everything.

So, give them one good thing to think about, focus on and build on.

> *"That stat you had about promotions was really interesting, try adding more stats throughout."*
>
> *"You did a big pause naturally before that punch line that really brought it home; let's add some more pauses throughout your talk track."*

Even if they ask, *"Are you sure? What about … ?"*

While it won't make their performance perfect, I guarantee you that you will see an instant improvement both in their anxiety and their delivery.

And you will also build trust.

So, in time, as they get better and can refine their skills, then you can move to the more focused method.

And scene.

THE FOCUS METHOD

For those that are more experienced and need to start honing their skills, I highly recommend the method used to train barristers and courtroom advocates.

It provides a consistent approach to training that is repeatable and iterative.

Pioneered by George Hampel, the process limits feedback to *one* issue that needs to be improved and corrected to immediately elevate the speaker's presentation as a whole.

The approach keeps things simple and means you can foster a tangible improvement with one area of focus, making it easier to digest and not distracting from all the facts and figures the spokesperson is trying to internalize in preparation for the interview itself.

I promise what you'll find is an overall improvement in the whole delivery, and also not leave your spokesperson feeling battered and bruised.

It's done in six distinct and clear stages.

Headnote

Identify one specific aspect of the performance to be addressed.

* *Your headnote is 'expansion,' as I think you need to bring more examples out to make sure people understand the point as sometimes it sounded vague.*

Playback

Reproducing verbatim that aspect of the performance.

* *It happened a few points, but one specific example was you said, "Our business has grown tremendously in all geographies," but you didn't explain how or why.*

Reason

Explain why this is something that can be mproved/addressed.

* *It didn't feel tangible and wouldn't give me anything to quote or use in an article.*

Remedy

Explain how to improve this aspect of the performance.

* *Think of something illustrative for each point so you can give colour to each claim. What would you use for your first point?*

Demonstration

Demonstrating how to apply the remedy to the specific problem.

* *"Our business has grown tremendously in all geographies, most recently, for example, in Japan, where we ..."*

Replay

The trainee performs again, applying the remedy with a different part of their speech.

INTERVIEW-SPECIFIC PREP

In the time immediately before the interview, many media and comms pros forget that it is *their* job to make the spokesperson uncomfortable.

It's only by doing so and getting your spokesperson familiar and comfortable with the good, the bad and the ugly of a media interview that you get them prepared properly.

Many times people just ask *"Why are you so great?"* - type questions. That is no help.

Sports players simulate multiple real plays on the field so they get their muscle memory for when the real play comes.

Pull out your acting chops and prep your people like an interview.

One-to-one phone call:
sit back-to-back with your person

Two anchor broadcast interview:
have two people ask questions

Panel session:
set up a panel

And then if you know the journalist is really demanding and asks short, pointed questions, emulate it. If you know you have two anchors, one who's nice and one who's tough, emulate it.

Putting it bluntly, don't phone it in.

All of this is still your responsibility.

Get as real to the real thing as you can.

If they're doing the work to prep, so should you.

Candidly, anything less does a disservice to your spokesperson.

MASTERING THE QUESTION MATRIX

As you're getting your spokesperson ready, it's handy to draw yourself a quick matrix:

> *What are the three key messages you want them to land?*

Write them down.

> *What are the three topics that could be a challenge?*

Write them down.

This is what you will 'score' your spokesperson on.

Then jot down at *least* five different questions that will cover these topics, making sure you use the following five forms of questioning:

Closed, Open, Probing, Reflective, Leading

This will give you a pretty decent list of key questions for your spokesperson to tackle, covering a range of issues and in different styles.

This is what you need to get them in the right headspace.

And when they can hold their own on the issues that need covering, no matter how the question is asked, *then* they're ready.

The five forms of question:

Closed
Designed to obtain short and precise responses, ideal for fact-finding and narrowing down options for further questions:
You're the CEO, aren't you?

Open
Encouraging detailed and thoughtful responses, leading to a deeper conversation:
Why did you want to become CEO?

Probing
Seek comprehensive insights and are often used for research and interviews:
Tell me more about the process of becoming CEO?

Reflective
Introspective and reflective questions prompt self-analysis and personal growth:
What was the hardest part about becoming CEO?

Leading
Deliberately influencing the direction of discussions and usually inflammatory:
Lots of people say you're too young to be CEO, don't they?

DURING THE INTERVIEW

If you're in the room with your spokesperson at the time of the interview or in the studio, you have one job – remain unflappable.

Because the last thing your spokesperson needs is someone else going haywire when an awful question comes or panicking when there is a curveball or looking blankly when assistance is sought.

Be present. Take notes. Provide encouragement.

That is the job.

And whatever you do, don't permeate this awful habit PR pros have of frantically scribbling answers and thrusting them in front of your spokesperson throughout the discussion.

It's overwhelming. And if you've done your prep, it's totally unnecessary.

What I would recommend is agreeing on a simple system between you and your spokesperson.

My recommendation is simple:
1. In the few minutes before the interview, when you're doing final checks, agree what the three to five most important points are.

2. Write them down on a blank sheet in large capital letters so they're legible, and have it in front of both of you or visible on a flip chart.

3. Then if, and only if, necessary, indicate the particular point you think your spokesperson should land on.

In a properly prepared interview scenario, this is all that should be needed as backup.

Remember, your role is to support and encourage.

Agree a system, stick to it, remain unflappable.

PASSING THE BATON

I promise I'm not getting on a soapbox, but if I had *one* observation, it's that PR pros at the top of an organization often exclude the rest of the team (who probably prepared all the materials) from the interview prep because it's the CEO or whatever.

I'll confess. I've done it. Either because I thought it was a sensitive topic, or it's just better for the exec.

Instead, please reverse the thinking and find every opportunity to include another member of the team.

Don't overcrowd the room – that has the opposite effect. You don't need a mob.

It's probably just the person who reports directly to you, or the team member responsible for that part of the business – like your financial comms, or consumer person, what have you.

First, if you end up sick or incapacitated on the day of the interview, then the exec will be supported by someone who has gone through the prep session.

You're avoiding uncertainty and unfamiliarity.

Second, and this is the soapbox moment, I think as comms pros we don't spend enough time mentoring our teams. I really don't. There's too much redlining documents and email chains.

Media relations is a knowledge and skills profession.

> You only know how to pitch a story to a journalist by picking up the phone and doing it.
>
> You only know how to write a press release by doing it.
>
> You only know how to prep and coach an exec by doing it.

Bring them into the room. Include them.

Because by doing so, you're setting up both your team and *your* exec for success in the short and the long term.

AFTER THE INTERVIEW

After the interview has happened, those moments are not the time for detailed feedback.

If you're doing a series of interviews, you might want to (or be asked to) give a note or two.

> *"Did that anecdote make sense?"*

> *"Did I hit all the data points?"*

Of course, give some *brief, clear* and *helpful* advice for the next interview, and help correct any stats or factual issues that might not have been quite right.

But keep it limited.

Even if the interview wasn't perfect.

Otherwise save the longer feedback until later in the day, or in the days following.

The last thing you want to do, while your spokesperson is processing what's happened and what's to come, is a barrage of new information and suggestions.

As I said before, don't pander to them. Make sure any errors are corrected.

But you want your spokesperson to stay focused and in a good mindset.

I know this is something more old-school PR pros will disagree with me on.
Especially if the interview wasn't the best.

But guess what? When your spokesperson has an interview that wasn't great, they probably know it themselves.

Coming down on them like a ton of bricks with a laundry list of all the critiques and problems is only going to make them feel worse.

Save the more detailed and thorough feedback to when both they, and you, are in a better headspace and it will be more readily received.

And then do so using the methods set out in this book; don't turn it into a homework-marking exercise.

Your job is to support and instil confidence before, during and after the process.

NOTES FOR PROS
- CLOSING THOUGHTS

Communications is an incredible profession. One that I don't think is valued enough.

We live in a world where reputation is currency. And it starts with us.

Showing up well, polished and ready at all times is what makes each of us and the professional indispensable.

This means we have to be consistent, reliable, give well-reasoned advice, and above all, always have our spokesperson's back.

Sometimes this means pulling all-nighters to get materials ready or speeches rewritten.
Sometimes it means giving practical but candid advice that challenges the people we advise.
Sometimes it means making people uncomfortable beforehand, so they excel when they're in the spotlight.

That's the job. It's an incredible responsibility. But it's also an incredible opportunity.

Ultimately, if you get it right, then you will be the most trusted person in the room.

So, I'll leave you with this thought. And it's the best career advice I ever received, and nothing gives me more pride than passing it on:

> **Prepare for every meeting as though you might be asked to run it.**

And by that I mean whatever stage of your career you're at, however your organization positions comms within its structure, be ready to show up any day, any time.

If you know the agenda of a meeting, if you know the spokesperson's talk track for an interview, if you anticipate edits, if you have slides or notes to hand, you will do two things.

First, you will do the duty, which I believe exists for all comms professionals, to be as good and as prepared – if not better – than the spokespeople we support.

Second, the day WILL come, where your boss is late, or someone doesn't have their work in order, but you do. And when you show up prepped, people will notice.

Now, go and help your spokespeople be brilliant.

> **But more importantly, go make yourself utterly brilliant.**

FINAL THOUGHT

As I conclude, I'm reminded of the famous quote by
Winston Churchill:

> *"Now this is not the end. It is not even the beginning of the
> end. But it is, perhaps, the end of the beginning."*

So, what's next?

It will always be true that those who can express their ideas
with persuasion, conviction and clarity stand out as compelling
leaders and visionaries within their organizations and industries.

Importantly, what I hope this book has done – whether you read
one page or all of it – is dispel the mistaken belief that being good
at public speaking is an ability you either have or you don't.

Instead, I believe that being brilliant at presenting, pitching
and speaking to the media are skills based on tried and tested
principles that anyone can easily learn and apply.

This book is both the embodiment of that belief, and my way of
showing you how to do it.

Everything you need is right here in the pages of this book.

That's why this is the end of the beginning; I've taught you
all I know.

The only thing I can't do is speak for you.

Because, frankly, I don't want to.

Why not?

Because the whole reason for wanting to write this book in the first place was to teach and encourage as many people as possible that being good at public speaking is a learnable skill.

And because I want to watch *you* speak, because I want to share in *your* utter brilliance, and because I want you to be proud of *yourself* for applying the knowledge in this book and doing something you didn't know you could.

Which means, in conclusion, there is only one thing left for you to do: go speak.

Put this advice and these skills into practice.
Be brave and be open to making errors, building your skills as you do.
And have faith in yourself that any improvement, no matter how small, is still improvement.

Most of all, take everything you've learned from this book and go do amazing things.

Because, supported by the advice in this book and the belief I have in you, you now have everything *you* need to share *your* ideas with persuasion, conviction and clarity.

And I can't wait for the world to hear them.

— BT-L

ACKNOWLEDGEMENTS

To everyone who has let me train them, because it taught me how to do this well and gave me the inspiration to share this knowledge.

In alphabetical order only, the seven amazing humans who have been incredible communications partners and were hugely encouraging with my own career journey and the process of writing this book: Ahava-Shaffra Gray-Read, Elizabeth Randall, Emily Scheer, Kathy Krenger, Natalie Harding-Cooper, Stefanie Wong and Vivienne Hsu.

To Mark Gallagher and Oliver Foster of Pagefield for giving a lowly barrister a chance at the big boys' table, and for teaching me how to pitch an idea quicker than a smoke break.

Barney Thompson, Peter Eavis, Ellen Sheng, Francine Lacqua, Gabi Fonrouge and Gabriel Sanchez who all taught me about good journalism, and the efficacy of brilliant and balanced spokespeople insights.

To all the incredible barristers I've worked with who are the most tenacious advocates I've ever met, the best storytellers I've ever listened to and in turn taught me so much.

To Iain Morely, who's incredible book *The Devil's Advocate: A Short Polemic on How to Be Seriously Good in Court* was the foundation of both my legal and comms skills.

The editorial team at LID who helped bring all of this to life and encouraged me to blend my knowledge and experience with my authentic style of delivery and passion for teaching in the way I know best.

And to my friends and coworkers – including John and Malin Decker, Brian LaRose and Cat Kom, Martin and David, Lisa, Diana, Michele, Jimmy, Szczepanek, Debbie Felix, Michael and Eddie, and Ian – who gave their unwavering encouragement and support throughout this process.

ABOUT THE AUTHOR

Benjamin Thiele-Long began his career as a barrister, completing pupillage and tenancy at 2 King's Bench Walk and Furnival Chambers before joining the international law firm Pinsent Masons.

He later moved into PR and communications, with agency roles including Pagefield and Cognito in London and the United States. He was initially based in New York before moving to San Diego to lead Cognito's West Coast offering, working with founders and executives in the technology, professional services and finance sectors.

He was appointed Managing Director of Financial Communications for international PR and communications consultancy Ketchum, serving as a strategic advisor and presentation trainer to C-suites and boards of multinational businesses in the retail, technology, FMCG, hospitality, and financial services sectors. He most recently served as Petco's Chief ESG and Communications Officer based in California.

He now lives back in the UK with his family, to whom he owes so much for their unwavering support.